SURVIVAL
for Busy
WOMEN

EMILIE BARNES

HARVEST HOUSE PUBLISHERS
Eugene, Oregon 97402

SURVIVAL FOR BUSY WOMEN

Copyright © 1986 by Harvest House Publishers
Eugene, Oregon 97402

Library of Congress Catalog Card Number 85-082153
ISBN 0-89081-492-9

Printed in the United States of America.

Survival for Busy Women is dedicated to several very special women who have encouraged me in the spirit of Titus 2:3-5:

My beautiful mother, Irene, now home with the Lord. By her energetic, hard work, she showed me a true example of a Proverbs 31 woman.

My Auntie Syd who has loved me as a daughter, and who encouraged me to share my experiences and talents with others.

Gertie Barnes, my mother-in-law, from whom I've learned much, especially how to cook Southern fried chicken. She is the perfect mother-in-law, a woman who sets a godly example.

Florence Littauer, my friend and mentor. Without her love, teaching, and God's guidance, the More Hours in My Day ministry would never have happened.

Finally, this book is dedicated to all the women who feel hassled, hustled, and hurried. My prayer is that *Survival for Busy Women* will give you the hope to cope with life's pressures.

—Emilie Barnes

CONTENTS

EXHIBITS ─────

INTRODUCTION ────────

One Sunday after church service, my husband, Bob, and I were visiting with some friends. When one woman asked me about my "More Hours in My Day" ministry, I told her about some of the recent seminars I had conducted around the country. All of a sudden, a man who was listening in on our conversation grabbed my arm. "Emilie, we live in a cesspool," he complained. Thankfully, his wife was not within earshot as he told me, "My wife doesn't work. We have three children, two of them in school. Yet she says she doesn't have time to clean the house."

Do you think that's an isolated case? It isn't. In today's hectic society, men and women are so busy that often there is no time left to plan and execute the daily routines of life. So life is lived in a constant panic, trying to stay on top of house, family, and career.

With more women in the work force, there has never been a greater need for basic organizational skills in our homes. Kathy and Bob are a typical couple. Both work, and they have two children in elementary school. But Kathy wants to quit her job. She feels there are too many evenings when she is too tired to cook dinner, provide quality time for the children, do the laundry, and maintain the house.

One night as Kathy discussed her frustrations, Bob insisted that quitting her job was not an option. "If you stop working, how will we make the car payments?" he asked.

"Sell the car," Kathy snapped. "I can't keep this juggling act up any longer. I'm exhausted, and I'm not the woman God intends for me to be."

Kathy is fortunate to recognize her problem before it is too late. She may be able to quit working if her family adjusts their life-style. She is also considering part-time employment. However, many women have no choice but to work—it's a matter of survival. And besides, staying home is no guarantee that you will stay on top of everything, especially if you have young children and are involved in church and/or community activities.

If you can relate to any of these struggles, this book is for you. That's why we've named it *Survival for Busy Women*. This is not some theoretical exercise. Each chapter is designed to give you practical advice to help you organize your home as efficiently as possible. In the process you will save money, feel less pressure, and find more hours in your day to enjoy your family, job, and life in general.

Before we start, I wish to thank the many women who have written and shared so many helpful ideas. Some of your suggestions were incorporated into this book. A special thanks to Linda Risbrudt for the ideas contributed in Chapter 15, "Enjoying the Holidays."

Chapter 1

Recipe for Beating Stress

> *"A woman who fears the Lord is to be praised. Give her the reward she has earned, and let her works bring her praise at the city gate."*
>
> Proverbs 31:30 NIV

At the start of most of my seminars, I like to play a little game. I ask all of the women to stand up. Then I ask them a series of questions. If they can answer "no" after each question, they remain standing. The first time they answer "yes" they have to sit down. Here are the questions:

1) Did you leave an un- made bed at home?
2) Do you have a messy closet in your home?
3) Do you have a messy handbag?
4) Do you know what you're having for dinner five days from now?
5) Do you have dirty dishes sitting in your kitchen sink?
6) Could you find last year's income tax return and documentation in three minutes?
7) Did you kiss your husband before you (or he) left home?
8) Do you have one or more piles of paper

around your house—on top of the refrigerator, game table, kitchen counter, desk,
or on the floor?

By the time I'm done there's rarely even one lady still
standing. How did you do? Did you answer "no" to
six of the questions? How about four? Two? One? Don't
feel bad. We all understand the struggle to control our
lives. Don't despair; help is on the way!

It's pretty easy to formulate a recipe for stress. The
eight questions just cited are a good start. Here's an even
simpler one:

3 pounds of Hassles. Any of life's pressures or
traumas will do.

5 cups of Hustle. These are common everyday
demands and can be supplied by any family
member, neighbor, employer, children's club,
church duty, or committee responsibility.

7 tablespoons of Hurrieds. You can pick them
fresh, directly off your schedule, expectations, and
responsibilities.

Now stir them up and cook the mixture in the
oven of life's trials. Hassled, Hustled, and
Hurried—it's a fail-safe formula for a massive
serving of stress. Serves one for 24 hours a day,
seven days a week, 52 weeks a year. Unless spoiled
by organization.

But how can we get organized? It seems like today's
woman is putting on a juggling act. Most jugglers can
handle two or three balls or objects fairly well. It's
when we add one or two or even more balls that
juggling becomes interesting.

How many balls is today's woman juggling? She
began with herself—her appearance, family, school.

Then she added a second ball—her husband. And a third—her home. Then came the children. That's four, five, maybe even more balls. Sounds tough, doesn't it? Now throw in the biggie. The final ball called JOB.

How can we possibly keep all these balls going at once? It seems like they are dropping all around us and we're spending most of our energy picking up the ones we've dropped. And making sure we don't drop the biggie. For if we lose that job, how will we make the house payments, pay the orthodontist, or keep the kids in private school?

For a while, I was one of those fortunate few who seemed to have my life all together. I was happily married with two preschool children and no pressure to have to work. Then one day my sister-in-law abandoned my brother and their three preschool children. Bob and I became guardians of those three children and now I was ''juggling'' five children under the age of five.

That was 25 years ago, and I survived. I made it because I learned how to organize. I could have caved in under the stress and suffered a chaotic home, a frustrated husband, and undisciplined children. There were times when it seemed like it might all collapse. But I persevered by using time-tested organizational formulas. Today we're the proud parents of wonderful, full-grown children. And the organizational skills I've learned have led to a fruitful ministry and business for my husband and me.

Yes, there is a recipe for beating stress! It's called ORGANIZATION, and I'm glad to share it with one and all:

- 1 quality period of time with God each day
- 1 list of carefully-thought-through long-term and short-term goals
- 1 list of priority activities to direct you toward achieving those goals

- 1 monthly calendar
- 1 weekly schedule book
- 1 pad of daily schedules
- 10-25 (or more, as needed) boxes with lids
- 1 3x5 card file box
- Several packs of 3x5 cards of various colors
- 1 box of file folders
- Several large trash bags
- 1 pad of weekly menu planners
- Assorted jars, shoe boxes, pens, baskets, and trays as needed

Mix the ingredients liberally according to the instructions in this book. Season liberally with prayer.

The result will be an organized home and a happier woman whose "children arise and call her blessed; her husband also, and he praises her." That's the promise of Proverbs 31:28, and you could be the recipient of that blessing!

Are you ready to begin? Then let's not delay a moment longer in working toward a more organized you!

Chapter 2

Establishing the Target

> *"Forgetting what is behind and straining toward what is ahead, I press on toward the goal to win the prize for which God has called me heavenward in Christ Jesus."*
>
> Philippians 3:13,14 NIV

If we don't have a target, we can never know if we have hit or missed it. Much time is wasted because we don't know where we're going. If we want to succeed, we must adopt a goal-orientation to life.

Early in our marriage Bob and I felt it was important to set goals. We dreamed of the type of home and family we wanted. We realized that in order to achieve those dreams we needed a plan. That plan became the "Barnes Family Life Goals."

We talked often of those goals, and periodically we adjusted them as our lives changed. The biggest change came as we began to mature in our Christian faith. That's when our goals became more Christ-centered.

Goal-setting works because God is a goal-setter. He's stated His goals for us in the Bible. We're to love each other, obey His commands, take His message to the entire world—we could give many examples. Many of the characters in the Bible were goal-setters. Joseph stored food for seven years in order to feed Egypt during famine. Moses led the Israelites out of Egypt. Jesus came to provide us with the way to eternal life. Paul desired to "know Christ and the power of his resurrection and the fellowship of sharing in his sufferings, becoming like him in his death" (Philippians 3:10 NIV).

No army can win a war without goals. Companies set goals and plan strategy in light of those goals if they want to be profitable. No football team would think of taking the field without a game plan. And so it is with individuals. People who set goals are people who succeed. They are the ones who tax themselves to reach their full potential. They are the ones who find life exciting, who are confident and have a sense of accomplishment.

Goals do not dwell on the past, for good planning can virtually erase the errors of the past. Goals are access lines to the future. They allow us to run the race with the finish line firmly established.

Goal-setting doesn't just happen. We must take time to think long-range in order to effectively plan for the next few days. And our goals must be important enough to work at making them happen. Bob and I have set ten-year goals, and then we've broken those down into smaller goals. Where do we want to be in five years if we're to fulfill our ten-year goals? What about three years? One year? Six months? Three months? One month? Today?

See the progression? How can we plan today if we don't know where we're headed? Sure, we can fill our time with activities; that's easy. But by goal-setting, everything we do is directed toward a purpose that we've set. If my goal for this year is to read ten books, then what book will I read first? If I want to disciple my family, what activities am I going to do? In Exhibit A, you can see how one woman does this. She breaks

ONE WOMAN'S
THREE-MONTH GOALS

	Jan. - Feb. - March		
	Activity Period		

Objectives		Target Date	Goals Realized
Personal			
1. Read: Loving God by Colson		2/1	1/18
2. Lose 5 pounds		3/1	3/6
Family			
1. Have a short devotion at breakfast		1/1	
2. Be a blessing to each other		1/1	
Career			
1. Enroll in "Elementary Accounting" at Local College		1/6	1/6
2. Apply for new position opening at work		1/15	1/15
Church			
1. Volunteer to be an usher		1/9	1/10

her goals for the year into three-month portions, sets a target date, and has space to record when the goal is achieved. So she wrote "Read *Loving God* by Chuck Colson" and planned to finish it by February 1. She achieved that goal ahead of schedule, on January 18. In this way, she breaks her long-range goals into small, bite-sized pieces.

One of my long-term personal goals is to mature as a Christian woman. How would that translate into specific goals? Two ten-year goals might be to be prepared to teach and lead a women's Bible study, and to write and publish a book relating to the fulfillment we can have as godly women. Five-year goal activities would be to teach a small group of young married women, to read materials relating to growth for godly women, and to make notes and clip materials relating to the future book. Three-year goal activities include assisting an adult Bible study teacher, attending seminars and workshops that relate to Christian growth among women, and reading materials that relate to this topic. One-year goals might be to attend a teachers' workshop and complete a creative writing class at the local community college. And today's goal activities are to spend time in prayer about my personal growth goals, to sign up for the creative writing class, to sign up for next month's beginner's teaching class at church, and to purchase colored file folders and begin a set of files relating to Christian characteristics that lead to maturity.

In the pages that follow I've listed several goals in areas such as Family, Spiritual, Material, Career, Physical, Recreational, and Financial. If our long-term desire is to become the women God wants us to be, we will be organized in every area of our lives. So for each area I've listed possible goal activities for one, three, five, and ten years, and activities for today in light of those goals.

Take, for example, the goal to raise children who are responsible for their behavior. Ten-year goals could include having teenage children with proper manners, proper respect for authority, and able to carry on an interesting conversation with adults. You can see that in order to reach those ten-year goals, there are specific five-, three-, and one-year goals. And there are specific activities planned for today in light of those goals.

The accomplishment of these smaller bites is what permits us to arrive at our long-range goals. They are road maps for life. They are not cast in concrete. They are flexible and can be ever-changing. However, they help us determine the target. In each of the categories, there are many goals and activities other than the examples stated. However, those listed give a few ideas of how we can begin putting our goals into action.

AREA: Personal
GOAL: To mature as a Christian woman

ACTIVITIES FOR REACHING THE GOAL:

Ten-Year Goal Activities
1. To be prepared to teach and lead women's Bible study.
2. To write and publish books relating to women's fulfillment as a godly woman.

Five-Year Goal Activities
1. To teach a small group of young married women.
2. To read materials relating to growth for godly women.
3. To make notes and clip materials relating to my future book.

Three-Year Goal Activities
1. To be an assistant to one of our adult Bible teachers.

2. To attend seminars and workshops relating to Christian growth among women.
3. To read materials relating to growth for godly women.
4. To make notes and clip materials relating to my future book.

One-Year Goal Activities
1. To attend future teachers workshop.
2. To enroll in a "creative writing" class at the local community college.
3. To begin a set of colored files to compile articles that are cut out as relating to Christian characteristics that lead to maturity.

Today's Goal Activities
1. To sign up for a "creative writing" class.
2. To sign up for beginners teaching class at church that begins in October.
3. To go to local stationery store to purchase colored file folders.
4. To spend time in prayer asking God for direction in my long-range goals that relate to my personal growth.

AREA: <u>Family</u>
GOAL: To have children responsible for their behavior

ACTIVITIES FOR REACHING THE GOAL:

Ten-Year Goal Activities
1. To have two teenage children with proper manners.
2. To have two teenage children with proper respect for authority.
3. To have two teenage children who can carry on an interesting conversation with adults.

Five-Year Goal Activities

1. To have two children who can exhibit proper manners in meeting people, eating out in restaurants, meal etiquette at home.
2. To have two children who can stand on their own convictions and who are willing to pay the price for their behavior.
3. To have two children who sit in with adults and discuss contemporary topics relating to current events.

Three-Year Goal Activities

1. To attend a training session on how to have proper etiquette in social graces.
2. To encourage the children to share in planning the menus, shopping for the food at the market, and to assist in the preparation of the meals.
3. To encourage the children to be part of the family decision-making process.

One-Year Goal Activities

1. To assist mother with the party invitations. Shop for the proper invitations, assist with party list, apply the postage stamps to the envelopes.
2. To set the table for the daily meals; including the center piece, candles, utensil placement, placemats, napkins, etc.
3. To plan the weekly agenda for our weekly "family conference."

Today's Goal Activities

1. To show proper introduction manners when the guests arrive for the potluck.
2. To assist Mom in bringing the food to the counter when guests bring their food for our party.
3. To ask the children to be sure to talk with the guests this evening.

AREA: Spiritual
GOAL: To learn how to share my faith with others

ACTIVITIES FOR REACHING THE GOAL:

Ten-Year Goal Activities

1. To be able to conduct seminars and workshops dealing with "personal evangelism."
2. To publish materials relating to sharing my faith with those in need.
3. To train others in sharing their faith by having a life-style that reflects the love of Christ.

Five-Year Goal Activities

1. To teach a small group of young ladies in the Sunday school group how to share Christ through their life-style.
2. To gather data and information sharing how others share their faith.
3. To read materials relating to life-style evangelism.
4. To make notes and clip materials relating to my future syllabus and speaking engagements.

Three-Year Goal Activities

1. To assist one of the ladies who teaches the evangelism class at church.
2. To attend the InterVarsity workshop at the local university dealing with sharing of one's faith.
3. To read all I can on the topic of witnessing.

One-Year Goal Activities

1. To attend witnessing class at church.
2. To attend Campus Crusade "Four Spiritual Laws" conference.
3. To enroll in "creative writing class" at local community college.

Today's Goal Activities

1. To invite my neighbor over for a cup of coffee (decaffeinated) and share about those things we have in common, i.e. children, school, husbands, meal planning, etc.
2. To send out invitations for three couples in our neighborhood to next month's potluck in our home.
3. To go to the local Bible bookstore and purchase a new book on the bestsellers list.

AREA: Material
GOAL: To build a home on one acre of land with 2500 square feet and four bedrooms

ACTIVITIES FOR REACHING THE GOAL:

Ten-Year Goal Activities

1. To move into our dream home.
2. To plant the landscaping with our favorite shrubs and trees.
3. To have a first mortgage of $90,000 with payments of no more than $1,200 per month with a 15-year loan.

Five-Year Goal Activities

1. To purchase our one-acre parcel and begin a five-year payment plan.
2. To begin to identify a reputable architect and contractor in our area.
3. To continue to select and clip from magazines those renderings that we would consider for our home.

Three-Year Goal Activities

1. To talk with couples who have designed and built their own homes.

2. To research the geographic area in which to purchase our one-acre lot.
3. To go to home-builder conventions to see the latest in building materials.

One-Year Goal Activities

1. To meet with the bank to determine a savings plan that will let us meet our financial goals relating to our building our own home.
2. To subscribe to two design magazines that preview our style of home.
3. To meet with the total family to discuss our goals for a new home. Also, review the sacrifices that will need to be made over the next few years in order to accomplish our goal.

Today's Goal Activities

1. To make an appointment to meet with the loan officer of our main branch bank.
2. To visit the main library and talk to the librarian about her recommendation of the two best architect magazines for our style of living.
3. To sit down and talk with the children about how they can help us with this plan.

AREA: Professional/Educational
GOALS: My goals for these are listed under Personal and Spiritual goals for my life. These will include many of the same activities that relate to these two areas. However, if I want to include additional classes, workshops, and seminars I would certainly want to list them and work toward their accomplishment.

AREA: Career
GOAL: To found a small ministry/business to share

Christ with women and families through life-style evangelism.

ACTIVITIES FOR REACHING THE GOAL:

Ten-Year Goal Activities

1. To speak, write, and publish through "ABC Ministries."
2. For "ABC Ministries" to be recognized in the Christian and secular community as training individuals how to live in peace and harmony with others in their homes, churches, professional lives, and communities.

Five-Year Goal Activities

1. To write and speak at every opportunity related to my topic of interest.
2. To read and clip all materials that will give me a basis from which to speak and write.
3. To interview those I meet who exemplify quality life-styles, to take notes and journalize for future speeches and writings.

Three-Year Goal Activities

1. To observe those individuals and families which reflect good, wholesome life-styles.
2. To attend seminars and workshops that deal with my topic of interest.
3. To assist in public speaking at church and civic groups.

One-Year Goal Activities

1. To sign up for Toastmaster's Club.
2. To begin to evaluate my life-style to see if someone would want to follow me.
3. To search Scripture to see what is written about life-style living.

Today's Goal Activities

1. Call the local Toastmaster's Club and find out how to join one of their groups.
2. Think through and identify one or two individuals who live a quality life that reflects positive Christian examples.
3. Begin reading the Book of John to study Jesus' life-style.

AREA: Physical
GOAL: To have my weight at 116 pounds

ACTIVITIES FOR REACHING THE GOAL:

Ten-Year Goal Activities

1. To have a well-balanced nutritional diet that maximizes my energies.
2. To maintain a low sodium intake.
3. To minimize the intake of sugar in my diet.

Five-Year Goal Activities

1. To continue to read the nutritional literature dealing with weight control.
2. To continue to listen to speakers who talk on healthful living.
3. To be aware of new research findings on good health.

Three-Year Goal Activities

1. To have a benchmark weight of no more than 112 pounds.
2. To eliminate refined wheat (substitute whole grains) from my family's diet.
3. To be involved in an aerobics class at the YWCA.

One-Year Goal Activities

1. To switch from regular coffee to decaffeinated coffee.

2. To evaluate my consumption of desserts and begin to minimize.
3. To switch from syrups with sugars to raw maple syrup.

Today's Goal Activities
1. To call the YWCA to find out about their aerobics classes.
2. To visit the local health food store and discuss with them current health trends.
3. To subscribe to a good nutritional magazine.

AREA: <u>Recreational</u>
GOAL: To be able to take a three-week vacation with the family

ACTIVITIES FOR REACHING THE GOAL:

Ten-Year Goal Activities
1. To enjoy a vacation with the family that utilizes all we've learned over the nine previous years.
2. To use this trip to plan, chart, and estimate the who, what, when, and where of this trip.
3. To use this trip to have the children use their math, science, health, and history skills to plan and execute this trip.

Five-Year Goal Activities
1. To plan a two-week vacation in the Sierra Nevada mountains hiking, camping, and fishing.
2. To assign each of the family members a certain area of responsibility to research, recommend, and plan.
3. To initiate selection of location for the ten-year destination.

Three-Year Goal Activities
1. To plan a one-week vacation at the beach.

2. The family would plan the details of the trip.
3. The children would begin to save part of their allowance for this trip.

One-Year Goal Activities
1. To plan several weekend trips to the ocean, mountains, and desert.
2. The family would plan details for these outings.
3. The children would help plan and shop for the food.

Today's Goal Activities
1. To purchase a qualified camping/vacation magazine that describes various planning aspects for successful vacations.
2. To go to the Automobile Club to acquire various maps showing details for our mini-vacations.

AREA: <u>Financial</u>
GOAL: To be able to build our dream home and to finance our three-week vacation

ACTIVITIES FOR REACHING THE GOAL:

Ten-Year Goal Activities
1. To move into our 2500-square-foot three-bedroom home on one acre of land with mortgage of $90,000 with no more than $1,200 monthly payment.
2. To enjoy a three-week vacation with the family with no more than $500 being financed for this this trip.

Five-Year Goal Activities
1. To purchase our one-acre parcel and begin a five-year payment plan.

self-sacrifice to our goals, then we can experience the satisfaction of success.

But what do we do when we have several steps to accomplish in reaching our goals? What do we do first? That's where our priorities come in. . . .

Chapter 3

Priorities—What Comes First?

"But seek first His Kingdom and His righteousness; and all these things shall be added to you."

Matthew 6:33 NASB

Jean had set her goals and organized her days according to those goals. But she never was able to complete her daily "To Do" list. "For example, I've got this pile of junk mail on my desk," she complained. "I never have time to go through it, so the pile just gets bigger and bigger."

I asked Jean to show me a typical list of her day's priorities. Here is what she jotted down:

1. Review junk mail
2. Get a haircut
3. Write four letters
4. Make bank deposit
5. Pay bills
6. Attend Bible study at neighbor's home
7. Have lunch with Mary Jane
8. Attend aerobics class
9. Pray 15 minutes as part of prayer chain

10. Clean house (two hours)
11. Purchase paint for weekend project
12. Watch Billy's Little League game at 6:30
13. Prepare chicken dinner for family
14. Solicit door-to-door for United Fund
15. Accept invitation for Saturday's potluck dinner
16. Begin planning for Mary's birthday party

The first thing Jean admitted was that she could not possibly do every one of those activities. She needed to process these options into three categories:

- YES: I will do this.
- MAYBE: I will do this if there is time.
- NO: I will not attempt this today.

Notice the last option? We must learn to say "NO!" Too many women assume that their only options are "yes" or "maybe." If we can't say "no" to some things, we become overcommitted and wind up carrying heavy loads of guilt for unfulfilled commitments.

The first time through the list, some of the YES decisions were obvious. Jean needed to make a deposit at the bank, fix dinner for her family, and attend her son's baseball game. Most of the others were not so clearcut. She didn't see any obvious "no's." She needed a system to help her choose between alternatives.

Making Decisions Using Priorities

Just how does a Christian proceed with decisions where the answer is not obvious? The diagram on the next page can help make such decisions easier.

Priority #1—God: According to Matthew 6:33, our first priority is to seek and know God. This is a lifelong pursuit. When God has first place in our lives, deciding among the other alternatives is easier. We are better able to decide what to read, what to view, how to spend our money, and where to give our time when

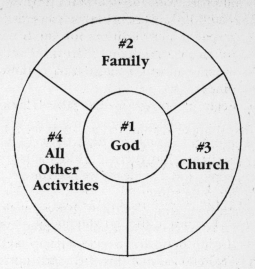

our thoughts are fixed on what is true, good, and right.

When I feel hassled, hustled, and hurried, it's often because this priority is out of order. Usually I need to adjust my schedule in order to spend time with God. When I allow Him to fill my heart, I relax and have a clearer perspective on the rest of my activities.

Priority #2—Family: In Proverbs we read about the woman who "watches carefully all that goes on throughout her household, and is never lazy. Her children stand and bless her; so does her husband. He praises her with these words: 'There are many fine women in the world, but you are the best of them all!' " (Proverbs 31:27-29 TLB).

How does a woman receive such praise from her family? By providing a home setting full of warmth, love, and respect. Creative moms provide quality time, touching, prayer, and eye contact for each family member. This family seldom questions Mom's commitment to them.

Priority #3—Church-Related Activities: Hebrews

10:25 tells us to be involved in our church, but that is not at the expense of the first two priorities. Actually, when the first two priorities are in order, there is plenty of time to participate in this important area of our lives. But occasionally, there may be weeks where church activities are minimized to allow us to focus on the first two priorities.

Priority #4—All Other Areas: This includes job, athletics, exercise, classes, clubs, and other activities. Some people find it amazing that there is time for any of these items. But there is. God wants us to be balanced people, and that means we need time for work and time for recreation.

You might be asking, "Is there really any time for me?" Yes! It is necessary that you take time for yourself. You are no good to anyone when you are exhausted, frazzled, hassled, hustled, and hurried. So occasionally you need to do your family a favor and give yourself time to cut some flowers, drink a cup of tea, read a book in a quiet place, take a nap, enjoy a hot bath, paint your nails, visit the beauty shop, or go shopping with a friend. These activities can revitalize you for the activities of home and church.

With these priorities in mind, Jean attacked her list of activities, beginning with the junk mail. "I think I'll just toss the whole pile!" she said. When she was done, her list looked like this:

Jean's Priorities for June 1

Activity	Action-Option
1. Open junk mail	NO—Toss
2. Get a haircut	YES
3. Write four letters	YES
4. Make bank deposit	YES

5. Pay bills	YES
6. Attend Bible study at neighbor's home	MAYBE
7. Have lunch with Mary Jane	MAYBE
8. Attend aerobics class	MAYBE
9. Pray 15 minutes as part of prayer chain	YES
10. Clean house (two hours)	YES
11. Purchase paint for weekend project	MAYBE
12. Watch Billy's Little League game at 6:30	YES
13. Prepare chicken dinner for family	YES
14. Solicit door-to-door for United Fund	NO
15. Accept invitation for Saturday's potluck	NO
16. Begin planning for Mary's birthday party	YES

By eliminating three activities and putting four more in the "maybe" category, Jean was immediately more relaxed. I encouraged her to cross off the "Yes" activities as she completed each one to give herself the satisfaction of seeing the list shrink during the day. If time permitted, she could do the "maybe" activities, but if she didn't, some of them might become "yes" activities on another day.

I also encouraged Jean to realize that there may be creative alternatives to some of her activities. For instance, attending a Bible study could be a priority, but she might need to find one that better fits her schedule and family commitments. She might find it to her advantage to fix several meals at once so she wouldn't be in the kitchen for long stretches every day. And there might be some activities that could be delegated to someone else.

Of course, not all decisions can be made so quickly. When evaluating priorities, there are some decisons that may take days or weeks. How does a Christian decide on those priorities when the answer is not obvious? I've made Paul Little's five-point outline from his booklet *Affirming the Will of God* (Inter-Varsity) my criteria when I face that kind of situation:

1) Pray, with an attitude of obedience to God. God's promise to us is, "I will instruct you and teach you in the way you should go; I will counsel you and watch over you" (Psalm 32:8 NIV).

2) Look for guidance from Scripture. What does the Bible say that might guide me in making the decision? "Be diligent to present yourself approved to God as a workman...handling accurately the word of truth" (2 Timothy 2:15 NASB).

3) Obtain information from competent sources in order to gain all the pertinent facts. "A wise man's heart directs him toward the right" (Ecclesiastes 10:2 NASB).

4) Obtain advice from people knowledgeable about the issue. It's best if our counselors are fellow Christians who can pray with and for us. "Iron sharpens iron, so one man sharpens another" (Proverbs 27:17 NASB).

5) Make the decision without second-guessing God. "...he who trusts in the Lord will prosper" (Proverbs 28:25 NASB).

Planning of our daily and weekly calendar is much easier once we've established long-range goals. They help us choose which alternatives to say "no" to as we realize that some activities don't fit into our mission plans. What we want to do is minimize the number of *good* things in order to concentrate on doing the *best* things in life.

If you're still not sure about your priorities, I suggest you take a few minutes with a piece of paper and write down everything you did yesterday (if that wasn't a typical day, pick the most recent one that was) and the time you took to do it. Start from the moment you got up in the morning and end with the time you went to bed that night. In addition to that exercise, answer the following questions:

1) How long do you spend in Bible study each day?
2) How much time do you spend in prayer (worship, thanksgiving, intercession)?
3) How long does it take you to put on your makeup?
4) How much time do you spend watching television each week?
5) How much time do you spend in casual conversation on the phone?
6) When was the last time you did something charitable (unrequired giving of time, energy, or substance) for your husband, child(ren), or a friend?
7) Would you be ashamed to have someone see your home as it is at *this* moment? How about on an average day?
8) When was the last time you gave witness to your faith in Christ?
9) (For mothers of preschoolers) When was the last time you took a day for yourself?

Now look over your paper and see how this measures up to God's priorities. Write down one thing you will do *beginning this week* to adjust those priorities.

Establishing priorities is a critical way to beat stress. In fact, it might even save your life. One woman wrote me this note a week after attending my seminar:

> I had an unsuccessful suicide attempt about two months ago. I've struggled lately with a depressed state. But after your seminar I have a new lease on life. I'm motivated and my attitude has greatly improved. Your section on priorities really ministered to me.

The purpose of having priorities is so we won't become overextended. Most of us do a lot of good things. But are they the best? If we know we're always doing the most important activities first, we can relax even when we can't complete everything on our "To Do" lists.

On Your Way to the Organized You!

After I finished a seminar on how to organize a household, a young mother rushed forward to tell me, "I loved all the organizational ideas and tips you gave for the family and home. But what about *me*? How do *I* get organized?"

I pulled my Daily Planner out of my purse. This is a tool I have used for years to get me through each day, week, month, and year of my life. I would be lost without it.

Organization really starts with our own personal lives. Once we have organized ourselves, we can move more confidently into the other areas of our lives such as our family, home, or job.

Here are the tools you need to get started:

- A purse-size binder with paper 5 1/2" x 8 1/2" or smaller
- Blank tabs that you can label yourself
- A calendar

The following are some of the ways I've labeled my tabs:

Goals

This is where the goals and priorities we've set are put into action. The procedure I've chosen allows me to write down the goal, the date I want to see it achieved, and intermediate steps necessary to reach that goal.

Let's see how Jane has organized her Daily Planner. In Exhibit B on the following page you can see three of Jane's goals for 1986. First is that she wants to revise her will. Note that she wrote the goal on January second and the deadline she set for completion was March 1. The first step was to call her lawyer for an appointment, which she did on the second. The second step was the actual appointment itself. There is also a place to write one or more considerations. In this case, Jane was considering the purchase of a new life insurance policy.

Another goal Jane set was to lose five pounds by February 15. The steps were to join an aerobics class, eliminate sugar from her diet, and get a physical exam. Note the column to check off each step as it is completed, so Jane can actually chart her progress.

Jane's third goal was spiritual—to join a women's Bible study. She needed to consider the children's school schedule, and with that in mind she called the church office to find out her options.

Your goals can be in any area, but be careful not to set too many at once. You might want to prioritize them with an "A" for most important, "B," or "C." Areas you might consider for goals are Scripture reading, prayer time, family, household, financial, budget, and career.

GOALS

TIME PERIOD	DATE

GOAL: I will revise my will by March 1st   **PRIORITY:** A

CONSIDER: New life insurance - dependents

No.	STEPS	DATE	✔
1	Call for Appointment	1/2	✔
2	Appointment at 10:00 for 2/3		

GOAL: I will lose 5 lbs. by February 15   **PRIORITY:** A

CONSIDER: Have a physical/checkup by doctor

No.	STEPS	DATE	✔
1.	Join an Aerobics Class	1/3	✔
2.	Begin Jan 6th	1/3	
3.	Modify my eating habits A. Eliminate sugar	1/4	
4.	Physical exam - Jan. 9th 9:00	1/4	

GOAL: I will join a Women's Bible Study

PRIORITY:

CONSIDER: Children's School Schedule

No.	STEPS	DATE	✔
1.	Call Church Office for schedule	1/4	✔
2.	Class begins January 14th at 10 A.M.	1/4	

Calendar

Purchase a small month-at-a-glance calendar at a stationery store and insert it into your binder. This allows you to quickly view all your commitments. Notice on Exhibit C that Jane wrote down her aerobics commitment at 9:00 A.M. on Mondays, Wednesdays, and Fridays, and her Tuesday-morning Bible studies. I put all my appointments, family, and church functions on this page.

Daily Schedule

This section allows us to more fully plan our day. We list our appointments as well as the things we wish to accomplish that day, rated by priority A, B, or C. Exhibit D is Jane's schedule for Monday, May 5. On the monthly calendar, she listed her three main appointments. Those three appointments go on the left-hand side of the page by the appropriate time. She has also scheduled time for devotions at 6:30. Then she's listed various things she needs to do under "Action List." There is a place to check off each item as it is completed.

This tool is useful for the mother who works outside her home as well as the homemaker who wants to get her daily household duties done in a more orderly manner.

To Do, To Buy

This is a place to note of all the things we need to do on an errand day. There may be some things we can't schedule on our daily planner. Rather than transferring the same list day after day, put them all in one place. I put down things like:

- Pick up winter coat at the cleaners

CALENDAR

MONTH May _____ YEAR _____

SUNDAY	MONDAY	TUESDAY	WEDNESDAY	THURSDAY	FRIDAY	SATURDAY
				1	**2**	**3** Part-I Seminar Orange 9:00-12:00
4 Church Brunch - Bosman's	**5** Hair Cut 10:00 Lunch-Barb P. Car Pool-3:00	**6** Bible Study 10:00-11:30 Carpool-3:00	**7** Car Pool 3:00 Little League Game 6:00	**8** Help at school 8:00-12:00 Car Pool-3:00	**9** Help at School 8:00-12:00 Car Pool-3:00	**10** Picnic at Beach
11 Church Complin's Brunch	**12** Aerobics Begins 9:00-10:00	**13** Bible Study 10:00-11:30	**14** Aerobics 9:00-10:00	**15**	**16** Aerobics 9:00-10:00	**17**
18 Church	**19** Aerobics 9:00-10:00	**20** Bible Study 10:00-11:30	**21** Aerobics 9:00-10:00 Christine's Teacher Conf. 2:45	**22** Dentist 11:00	**23** Aerobics 9:00-10:00	**24** Garage Clean out
25 Church	**26** Aerobics 9:00-10:00	**27** Bible Study 10:00-11:30	**28** Aerobics 9:00-10:00	**29**	**30** Aerobics 9:00-10:00	**31** Garage Sale 8:00-2:00 Family BBQ

DAILY SCHEDULE

MON TUE WED THU FRI SAT SUN	May 5 DATE

TIME	APPOINTMENTS	ACTION LIST TO DO/TO BUY	PRIORITY A B C ✔
6			
7	Devotion Time		
8		Call Women's Chrm.	A ✔
9		Take clothes to cleaners	A
10	Hair Cut		
11			
NOON	Barbara D. Back-Street	Go to Hardware for Husband	B ✔
1			
2			
3	Car Pool	Go by Dairy	A ✔
4			
5			
6			
7		See that Chad does Science	A ✔
8		Hem Blue Dress	B
9		Read New Book	B

- Shop for new pair of shoes
- Stop by the library

Notes

This is a place to write down notes from speakers you hear, or to capture important points at meetings, Bible studies, or sudden ideas for a project that pop into your mind at the most surprising times. I use this section to record notes from the sermon every Sunday morning (Exhibit E).

Miscellaneous

This is where I keep topical lists such as:

- Emergency phone numbers
- Dentist/physician
- Baby-sitters' phone numbers
- Favorite restaurant phone numbers
- Books and music recommended

You may want to label some of these areas separately rather than putting them all under one tab. Two things I include in this section are "Communication Log" (Exhibit F) and "Sources" (Exhibit G). In the first, I keep an ongoing record of communications with key individuals. The example you see is my communications with our insurance agent. The second category allows me to list important sources in various areas. This is a great way for sharing information with friends or quickly looking up address and phone numbers without always hauling out the Yellow Pages.

Expenses

This allows us to keep track of our expenditures for the month (Exhibit H). It includes:

- Date of expenditure

SERMON NOTES

DATE: May 4   **SPEAKER:**

TITLE: Choose For Yourself

TEXT: Joshua 24

Farewell address II —
A review of Israel's History

The pronoun "I" (God) is mentioned
17 x's.

Contrast between Israel & our growth
    A. History   vs. 4-5
    B. Birth of a nation   vs. 6-7
    C. Growth & Adolescence   vs. 8-10
    D. Mature Manhood   vs. 11-12
    E. Obedience   vs. 13
    F. Call for a decision   vs. 14-15
       (We all serve someone)
    G. Response of the people   vs. 16-18
    H. Warning by Joshua   vs. 19-24
    I. Joshua makes a covenant
       with the people   vs. 25-28
    J. Joshua dies   vs. 29

What is my decision?
Talents?   Faith?   Time?

COMMUNICATION LOG

PERSON/GROUP
Ken Barnes- Blue Shield

COMPANY: Fidelity Insurance   555-4710

ADDRESS: 12345 Willow St. #204

NOTE: Talk to Shirley Simcox

DATE	SUBJECT	✓
1/4	To submit Insurance claims	✓
1/15	Received letter needing Bob's signature-returned same day	✓
2/3	Received check for $205.74 Signed and sent to Hospital	✓
2/15	Need claim forms sent to me. Received 2/18	✓
2/26	ask Shirley to reduce our deductible from $500.00 to $250.00 —Will send rider ASAP— Received 3/14	✓
3/7	Ken called requesting clarification on upcoming physical exam — I wrote letter and mailed 3/9	✓

EXHIBIT F

SOURCES

CATEGORY
Interior Decorators

NAME/ADDRESS	TELEPHONE
Kim Design 17642 E. Jason St. Riverside, Ca. 92505	(714) 555-4372

COMMENTS/CONTACT
Does an Excellent job w/Early America.
See: Kim Green

NAME/ADDRESS	TELEPHONE
New Color Trends 703 E. 5th Way Newport Beach, Ca. 92660	(714) 555-4728

COMMENTS/CONTACT
The latest in Paint
& Wall Coverings.   See: Sue Beck

NAME/ADDRESS	TELEPHONE
The Carpet Mill 24316 Paddock Ln. Sunnymead, Ca. 92388	(714) 555-2748

COMMENTS/CONTACT
Good range of colors—
Good installation.   See: Joan Chamley

NAME/ADDRESS	TELEPHONE
Olson's Furniture 21623 Central Ave. Riverside, Ca. 92506	(714) 555-1206

COMMENTS/CONTACT
A great selection of
Period Furniture.   See: Harvey Olson

NAME/ADDRESS	TELEPHONE
Georianne's Floors & #23 Flower St. Windows Pasadena, Ca. 92503	(213) 555-2306

COMMENTS/CONTACT
A great buy on wooden
2" shutters.   See: Ann Peterson

EXPENSES

ITEMIZED

January				
MONTH/YEAR				

DATE	ITEM	CASH	CHECK	CREDIT CARD	AMOUNT	
1/2	Jim's Shoe Repair	☐	☑	☐	21	02
1/2	School Bus Ticket	☐	☑	☐	15	—
1/4	Market	☑	☐	☐	62	—
1/5	Babysitting	☑	☐	☐	5	75
1/6	Dairy	☐	☑	☐	18	63
1/7	Drycleaners	☑	☐	☐	6	85
1/7	Newspaper	☐	☑	☐	10	—
1/9	Market	☐	☑	☑	50	—
1/10	Allowances	☑	☐	☐	3	—
1/11	Gasoline	☐	☐	☑	18	25
1/12	Car Insurance	☐	☑	☐	123	64
1/14	Dental Bill	☐	☑	☐	50	—
1/15	Market	☐	☑	☐	36	—
1/16	Hallmark Cards	☑	☐	☐	6	05
1/17	City of Riverside	☐	☑	☐	73	26
1/19	Water Bill	☐	☑	☐	29	30
1/20	Haircut	☐	☑	☐	17	—
1/21	Lunch Out	☐	☐	☑	7	43
1/22	Dairy	☑	☐	☐	15	—
1/23	Gasoline	☐	☐	☑	21	13
1/25	Allowances	☑	☐	☐	3	—
1/28	Laundry	☐	☑	☐	14	—
1/29	Pictures	☑	☐	☐	7	24
1/29	Stage Play Tickets	☐	☑	☐	24	—
		☐	☐	☐		
		☐	☐	☐		
		☐	☐	☐		
		☐	☐	☐		
		☐	☐	☐		
		☐	☐	☐		
		☐	☐	☐		
		☐	☐	☐		
		TOTAL			730	57

- Item or service purchased
- Method of payment (cash, check, or credit card)
- Amount spent

If you have expenses related to your work or business, you will want to keep separate pages for home and work.

Prayer Requests

I have seven colored insert tabs for this section, one for each day of the week. On a comprehensive list of prayer requests, I write out the names of friends and family and divide them into five equal lists. One list is assigned to each day of the week, Monday through Friday. I leave Saturday as a swing day for immediate prayer requests. Sunday is open for prayer requests I learn of at church. I also write down Scripture from the pastor's sermon that can provide me with Scriptural content for my prayers.

On the sample from my prayer section (Exhibit I), you can see how I write down the date I receive a prayer request, the nature of the request, and any Scriptural promise I might claim. The far right column is labeled "Update/Answer Date." Recording the results of prayer and dates they were answered allows me to see how God has worked in my life and in the lives of my friends. Of course, not all prayers are immediately answered by "yes" or "no." Some are put on "hold" for a while. But seeing how God has answered the others encourages me to continue praying for the ones on "hold."

While "My Daily Planner" is a fantastic tool for me as I'm out and on the go, there are some things I need to organize but do not have to carry with me. So at home I keep a larger 8 1/2" x 11" notebook. I have

PRAYER REQUESTS

DATE	REQUEST	SCRIPTURE	UPDATE/ANSWER	DATE
1/8	Georgia's mother is sick		Out of Hospital	1/14
1/22	Brad's Escrow		Closed	1/24
1/29	Jennifer's Tooth		Dentist Filled	1/29
1/30	Offering at Church	Phil. 4:19	Met needs	2/5
2/3	Elder's Meeting	I Tim. 3:1-7	Went well	2/4
2/7	Thanks to God for answered Prayer	Mk. 11:24	Every day an answer	
2/14	Christine's Toilet Training		Going well	3/1
2/21	Craig's loan on his home	Matt 6:8	Approved	3/1
2/28	Mom's Trip to Texas		Great Trip	
3/2	Large Seminar in Northern Cal.	Phil. 4:13	Good Response	3/6
3/4	Aunt Gladys' Funeral		Isn't it good to be a christian?	3/4
3/6	Inter-Varsity Committee		Good Planning	3/7
3/10	Men's Prayer Breakfast		Four new men	3/10

EXHIBIT I

color-coded various pages (Exhibits J through N) for easy reference:

- **HOME INSTRUCTIONS (Exhibit J):** This is a weekly routine of chores and errands. A quick glance at it each day reminds me to do things like water the plants, set out the trash, and water the lawn.
- **FAMILY HOUSEHOLD EXPENDITURES (Exhibit K):** This is a more detailed accounting of our household finances than the one in "My Daily Planner." All the bills are recorded on here in 20 different categories. This makes it easy to establish and control a household budget.
- **IMPORTANT NUMBERS (Exhibit L):** This is a quick alphabetical reference for all important services, from ambulance to veterinarian.
- **FAMILY HISTORY (Exhibit M):** Do you have trouble remembering your husband's shirt size? Or the last time you got a tetanus shot? Here we can list each family member with blood type, dates of last doctor and dentist visits, innoculation dates, clothing sizes, and other interests (here's a place to put down gift ideas).
- **CREDIT CARDS (Exhibit N):** List each credit card, card number, company address and phone number, and the expiration date. If you ever lose your purse, you'll be glad you have all of this information in one place.

One last idea. It's not always convenient to be opening and closing a notebook. I keep a "Daily Reminder" pad in my kitchen. There are three columns on this bright yellow paper: "Call," "Do," and "See" (Exhibit O). This eye-catcher helps me accomplish the things I need to do each day, and I can tear it off the pad and take it with me.

HOME INSTRUCTIONS

DAY OF WEEK	ROUTINE CHORES/ERRANDS	SPECIAL APPOINTMENTS
SUNDAY	Christine & Chad's Sunday School Begins 9:45	Grandparents to take home after church
MONDAY	Water front plants Feed bird Bring in paper each morning	Chad's Dentist Appointment 2:30
TUESDAY	Set out trash	
WEDNESDAY	Water front lawn Feed bird	Mail off Letters, bills
THURSDAY	gardener comes today	
FRIDAY	Set out trash Feed bird	
SATURDAY	Water indoor plants	

EXHIBIT J

FAMILY HOUSEHOLD EXPENDITURES

MONTH OF January ___

HOUSE PAYMENT/RENT	FOOD	UTILITIES	FURNITURE/REPAIRS	CAR/GAS	INSURANCE	PHONE	CLOTHING	CLOTHING/HOUSE CLEANING	HAIRCUTS	SCHOOL EXPENSES
929.00	72.13	102.40	Car-76.02	21.00	427.00 Car	72.00	15.00	14.00	25.00	5.00
	50.76			17.50	170.00 Med	23.00	41.00	45.00	7.00	4.00
	39.00			18.00			16.00		4.50	3.75
	83.40			20.00			30.00		5.00	6.04
	24.24									
	62.43									
929.00 **TOTALS**	331.96	102.40	76.02	76.50	547.00	95.00	102.00	59.00	41.50	18.79

DEDUCTIBLE ITEMS

CREDIT CARD CHARGES	INVESTMENTS	MEDICAL/DENTAL	MEDICINES	BABYSITTING	TAXES	DONATIONS	SAVINGS	OTHER MISC. EXPENSES
47.00 B/A	60.00 Mutual Fund	25.00	18.00	—	225.00	175.00	100.00	60.00 United Way
								10.00 Booster Club
								10.00
								Boy Scouts
47.00 **TOTALS**	60.00	25.00	18.00		225.00	175.00	100.00	80.00

IMPORTANT NUMBERS

SERVICE PERSON	PHONE NUMBER	SERVICE PERSON	PHONE NUMBER
AMBULANCE	555-4203	NEIGHBOR - Sally	555-0011
APPLIANCE REPAIR	555-4219	NEWSPAPER	555-4738
DENTIST - Merrihew	555-4703	ORTHODONTIST	555-1104
DOCTOR - Turnbull	555-4909	PASTOR	555-0767
ELECTRICIAN - Rusty	555-1001	POISON CONTROL	555-0013
FIRE	555-9996	POLICE	555-5001
GARDENER - Mike	555-4618	POOL SERVICE	—
GAS CO. EMERGENCY	555-5551	PLUMBER	555-0114
GLASS REPAIR		SCHOOL(S) - Elem.	555-9013
HEATING/AIR COND. REPAIR PERSON	555-0013	SCHOOL(S) - Jr. High.	555-1111
HUSBAND'S WORK #	555-0321	VETERINARIAN:	—
INSURANCE (CAR)	555-0112	cat's name:	Tiger
INSURANCE (HOME)	555-0112	dog's name:	Mickie
		Animal Control	555-0014
		Security System	555-1163
		Trash	555-0731
		Newspaper Boy	555-0014

FAMILY HISTORY

FAMILY MEMBER NAME	BIRTH DATE	BLOOD TYPE	DATE OF LAST: YEARLY PHYSICAL	DENTAL EXAM	EYE EXAM	INNOCULATION/ DATE	OTHER
Christine	7/9/83	B	12/83	7/84	—	at 18mo.	
			12/84	1/85	—	DPT	
			1/85	6/85	—	RUBELLA	
				12/85	12/86	MEASLES	
Chad	11/20/84	B	12/15/85	—	—	6 MO. - DPT	
						POLIO 5/85	

FAMILY MEMBER NAME	SIZES DRESS/SUIT	SHOES	PANTS	SOCKS	UNDERWEAR	FAVORITE ACTIVITIES	OTHER CLUBS, INTEREST, ETC.
Christine		5	2T	Toddler		Puzzles,	Bible Stories,
Chad		3	12 MO	—	—	books, ponies,	singing
Craig	16½	9½ D	32"	9½	32	balloons	
Jenny	7	7½	7	B	Med		

CREDIT CARDS

If lost or stolen, notify company at once.

COMPANY	CARD NUMBER	COMPANY ADDRESS	COMPANY PHONE NUMBER	CARD EXPIRES (DATE)
BANK OF AMERICA		7264 Archibald St. San Francisco, CA 94100	555-8421	
SHELL OIL		1123 Sage Brush Phoenix, AZ 85012	565-3321	
American Express		62431 Hilltop Ln. Boston, MA 02106	555-4306	
Diners Club		2731 Hale Ave. Los Angeles, CA 90001	555-6626	

DAILY REMINDER

DATE: 5-14

Call:

1 Ben's Plumbing
  555-4221

2 Insurance - Car
  555-4702

3 Lamb School
  Jenny's Teacher

4 555-9990

5 Pastor Cook
  555-0233

Do:

1 Take clothes
  to cleaners

2 Car Pool driver
  this week

3 Take dinner
  to Merrihews

4 Visit Mrs. Jones
  at Hospital

5

See:

1 That Chad gets
  homework done

2 Hubby for
  lunch

3 Barbara D.
  at ballgame

4 That Christine's
  dress is hemmed

5 Focus on the family
  on T.V. @ 8:00 P.M.

Do you feel a little better now? If you just take an hour or two to invest in a "Daily Planner," you'll be removing a major cause of stress in your life. You'll be on your way to a more organized you!

Chapter 5

From Total Mess to Total Rest

"I can do all things through Christ, which strengtheneth me."

Philippians 4:13 KJV

Are you a pack rat? Before you answer, take this quick quiz. Give yourself one point for every "yes" and zero for every "no."

1. Do you find yourself complaining that you don't have enough room or space?
2. Do you have things piled up in cupboards and closets, or stacked into corners because there is no place to put them?
3. Do you have stacks of unread magazines around the house? (Are you saving them for that special day when. . .?)
4. Do things often get "lost" in your home?
5. Do you often think, "I'll just put this here for now and put it away later?"
6. Are things collecting on top of your refrigerator, counters, end tables, coffee tables, and bookshelves?
7. Do you have things you have not used for a

year, or possibly don't want, lying around the house?

8. Do you ever buy something you already have because you can't find it or don't want to take the time to search for it?

9. Do you often say, "This might come in handy someday?"

10. Do you have to move things around in your closets or cupboards to find a certain item?

Now total up your score.

0-3   Looks pretty good
4-7   Could use some improvement
8-10   It's never too late, Pack Rat!

If you'll follow through on the suggestions in this chapter, you will be amazed how better-organized your home will become. Sound incredible? That's why I quoted Philippians 4:13 at the beginning of this chapter. You *can* do all things *through Christ* who strengthens you. To show you how, we are going to break this huge task into bite-size pieces.

First, decide which area of clutter is bothering you most. The top of the refrigerator? The hall closet? The dresser drawers? That's where you'll begin the process we'll describe in a moment.

Second, set aside a 15-minute time slot to begin to take care of that clutter. Set your oven timer (or a portable hand timer if you are away from the kitchen area) and go to it. You will be surprised what you can accomplish in just 15 minutes. Sure, you won't finish today. But if you take 15 minutes a day for the next few weeks, attacking each area of clutter, you'll soon feel like you're living in a new house. And in the process, we're going to give you a system for keeping your home clutter-free! Plus, you will have a simple plan for keeping on top of the household routine.

The theme of this chapter is "Out of sight, out of mind." We're going to go through your house and throw away or give away anything you don't intend to use in the near future. Our motto is "When in doubt, throw it out."

Now don't panic. We're not going to throw everything away. But everything we do keep is going to be organized so we can find it in a moment. One woman told me that over a five-week period she organized her entire household into 135 cardboard boxes, each numbered and catalogued. "I'm a pack rat," she admitted, "but at least I'm an organized one!"

I believe 15 minutes a day for five weeks can do the job for most women. All of us can find a 15-minute time slot if we really try. That's why I suggest we set the timer each day for the duration of the project. We work like mad for the 15 minutes, then go back to whatever we were doing. Within a week, allowing for one day off, we'll have invested one hour and 30 minutes. Most of us can do a thorough cleaning of one room—including closets, dressers, under the beds—in that amount of time.

Equipment Needed

Are you ready? Let's begin first with the tools we'll need:

- 12-24 boxes (maybe more—remember the woman with 135 boxes), preferably white "perfect boxes"—16" long by 12" wide by 10" deep, with flip-top lids
- 1 black, felt-tip marking pen
- 1 3" x 5" card file box
- 3" x 5" cards of various colors, and dividers

- Package of 8½" x 11" colored file folders
- 1 file box
- 3 large trash bags (or maybe more, depending on the extent of the clutter)

Now what area of clutter did you identify as bothering you most? That's the room where we want to begin. (However, I suggest you don't start in the kitchen. Save that for the last week because you will need all the experience you can gain from doing the other rooms.) First, take the three trash bags and label them:

THROW AWAY
GIVE AWAY
PUT AWAY

For purposes of illustration, let's begin with the hall closet. Take everything out of that closet. Every item will require a decision and we need to be RUTHLESS. If you end up taking a couple of minutes trying to decide on each item, then call on a friend to help. She will help you make decisions you haven't been able to make for years because she is not emotionally involved with your possessions.

After everything is out of the hall closet, return only those items which actually belong in a hall closet—sweaters, coats, umbrellas, boots, football blanket, binoculars, tennis rackets, etc.

What do we do with all the other things that don't belong there? What about those old magazines we have collected for seven years? (That's right—we were going to thumb through them one rainy day and cut out the recipes.) What about those worn-out coats that have hung unused for five years? The baseball caps no one has ever worn? The board games? Old receipts and warranties? They all go in either the "Throw Away," "Give Away," or "Put Away" bag.

Everything that does not belong in the hall closet must go in one of the three bags. Make the decisions quickly. Usually our first impression is the right one.

Once we've completed the hall closet, we move on to the next room. As we systematically go through the house, over the next five weeks we will begin to fill our three bags. If one gets too full, start another.

At the end of the project, take the bag(s) labeled "Throw Away" and set them out for the trash man. They're gone! You'll be amazed how many things are out of the way.

Now we're left with two bags—"Give Away" and "Put Away." The Give Away bag(s) hold things that we might want to give to another family member (baby clothes or maternity clothes that are no longer needed). Or we might donate them to a thrift shop or church rummage sale or a missionary organization. Or perhaps we will want to cooperate with several others who have gone through this same process and have a garage sale. (More on garage sales in a later chapter.) Not only have we cleaned these items out of our house—they have been put to good use.

Storage

That leaves us with the Put Away bag. What do we have in it? Billy's first baby blanket. Some fabric scraps. A shirt our husband wore once to a special party. The possibilities are limitless. How are we going to organize all of this stuff?

It's time to get out those boxes and 3" x 5" cards.

One of the tabs in our 3" x 5" file box will be labeled "STORAGE." With our black felt-tip pen, we number our boxes, beginning with number one. Likewise, we label a 3" x 5" card to correspond to each box—"Box 1," "Box 2," "Box 3," and so on. As we place an item in a box, we write that item on the

appropriate 3" x 5" card. We keep going until every
item is placed in a box. Then we write on each card
where we are storing the box, so we can find it
quickly.

When you're done, each box should have a card that
looks something like this:

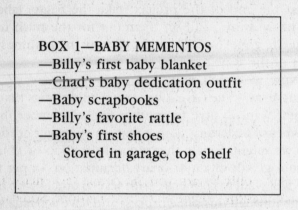

BOX 1—BABY MEMENTOS
—Billy's first baby blanket
—Chad's baby dedication outfit
—Baby scrapbooks
—Billy's favorite rattle
—Baby's first shoes
    Stored in garage, top shelf

One day our married daughter, Jenny, came by the
house with her friend Lynn. "Mom, Lynn and I are
making padded photo album covers. I was wondering
if we could use some of those remnant fabrics you've
stored away?" Jenny asked me.

I went over to my 3" x 5" file box, looked behind
the tab labeled "Storage," and found that fabric scraps
were in box number 28 which was stored in the garage.
We went out to the garage and pulled out the box, and
the whole process took only two minutes. Lynn
couldn't believe what she'd seen: "If I'd asked my mom
for fabric, she would have looked in ten or 20 boxes
and searched through closets all over our house trying to find what I needed." She added, "Mom would
have found it eventually, long after I'd found something
else instead."

Here are some of the kinds of boxes you might have labeled on your cards:

Box 1	Baby mementos
Box 2	Toys
Box 3	Summer clothes
Box 4	1984 tax information
Box 5	High school yearbooks
Box 6	Scrapbooks
Box 7	Old pictures
Box 8	Snow clothes
Box 9	Scrap fabrics
Box 25A	Christmas decorations—candles, holders
Box 25B	Christmas ornaments
Box 25C	Holiday tablecloths and napkins; poinsettia napkin rings

That's only a start; you, no doubt, have many more categories for storage. But we're not done. Some of the items in our Put Away bag don't belong in such boxes. We have old newspaper clippings, warranties, instruction booklets, receipts for major purchases, and so on. Now it's time to use our file folders. Here are some of the labels you might want to have on your folders:

1. Report cards
2. Appliance instructions
3. Warranties
4. Decorating ideas
5. Insurance papers and booklets
6. Special notes, letters, and cards
7. Car repair receipts
8. Receipts for major purchases

Some time ago, the icemaker on our refrigerator broke for the second time. When I asked the repairman how much it would cost to fix, he told me,

"Sixty-five dollars. However, I believe I repaired it six months ago, so it's under warranty if you can find the receipt." I went right to my file box, looked under "Repair Receipts," and found the required paper within 30 seconds. Then the repairman uttered these wonderful words: "Mrs. Barnes, you just saved yourself 65 bucks!"

Color-coding these files can help us find items even faster. Color is a universal shorthand. Some ways we can color-code our files are:

- By priority: Urgent is red, on hold is yellow, go is green.
- By individual: John is red, Cindy is blue, Christine is yellow.
- By subject: School records file is yellow, financial receipts file is green.
- By status: Active file is red, inactive is blue, cancelled or completed is black.

Household Routine

Now that we've got the house totally clean, how are we going to maintain it? Surely we never want to endure such a mess again.

Remember our rule: **"Don't put it down, put it away."** That alone will save stress. Just discipline yourself to handle an item once and put it directly away. If you have a two-story house, you might want to place a colored plastic container at the bottom of the stairs and another at the top of the stairs. Instead of making extra trips up and down the stairs, you can place items in the containers. When one is full, take it either up or down the stairs, sort and put away the contents, and replace the container in its proper location. This is especially helpful when you have young children who scatter toys from one end of the house to the other.

The primary way we maintain our "new" house is through our 3" x 5" card file. Take the dividers and label the tabs as follows:

1. Daily
2. Weekly
3. Monthly
4. Quarterly
5. Twice per year
6. Annual
7. Storage (You should already have this one completed.)

In the first section, we write down all the things we need to do daily. This would include such things as washing the dishes, making the beds, cleaning the bathrooms, and so on. This might seem elementary, yet it's amazing how many women don't make the bed or do other basic chores. It is very important to begin disciplining ourselves to a daily routine and this card(s) can serve as a checklist.

I was speaking at a women's retreat in southern California and a woman came up to me after a session, excited about what she had learned through my books. "They've changed my life," she gushed. When I asked her to give me an example, she said, "I grew up in a home where we *never* made our beds. We just threw three blankets on the mattress and crawled in. So I had to learn and now I'm teaching my family to make their beds. Also, I followed your five-week organizational plan and our house seems better organized and a lot neater. I look every day at my 'daily card' to help remind myself not to forget things like the bed."

Even though the daily cards may seem simplistic, they are important, especially in the beginning, to keep your maintenance program rolling. As you continue to check that card daily, you will establish new habits and soon it will become second nature.

In the "weekly" section of our card file, we write out those things we need to do once per week. We might have seven cards that look like this:

Monday—washing
Tuesday—ironing, water plants
Wednesday—mop floors
Thursday—vacuum, grocery shopping
Friday—change bed linens
Saturday—yard work
Sunday—plan next week's schedule, take a break

Now suppose it's Thursday and Linda, my closest friend, calls to suggest, "Mervin's is having a big sale today. Let's go shopping and have lunch together." I check my card for Thursday. I can do my grocery shopping this afternoon, but I don't know about the vacuuming. I accept the invitation and the vacuuming doesn't get done.

So what do I do? I can move that activity over to Friday. But Friday is a full day and so I would have to bump something to Saturday. But Saturday I have planned a picnic in the park with the kids. So I move it to Sunday, but that won't work either because we are going to church and we have company coming afterwards.

It seems that if we miss a day, we never catch up. So we break the vicious cycle. If we miss vacuuming on Thursday, that means we don't vacuum until *next* Thursday. In other words, we rotate our cards daily, whether we do the allotted jobs or not.

That may mean crunching on dirty carpet for a week. Some may protest, "I can't possibly do that." But this process disciplines us to keep our priorities in order. Next week if Linda calls again and says, "Let's go to lunch," I can say, "I'll go to lunch if I can get my vacuuming done, because if I don't do it, it means another week before I can do it."

This process allows us to be in control of our home, rather than having our home control us.

The next division is for our monthly activities. We might have cards that say things like this:

Week 1—Clean refrigerator
Week 2—Clean oven
Week 3—Mending
Week 4—Clean and dust baseboards

These are activities we can do any time during the week. Or we might delegate it to one of our children. To make sure it gets done, pull the card and put it on the refrigerator. In this way, every week we are doing a little bit to maintain our home and we don't have to endure a total mess again.

Then there are the quarterly activities. These might include such activities as straightening drawers, vacuuming the sofa and easy chairs, washing windows. Twice-a-year activities might be switching screens and storm windows or rearranging the furniture. Finally, there are activities we only need to do once a year, such as cleaning the basement, attic, or garage; cleaning the curtains and drapes; washing the carpets and walls. These cards are also rotated according to the time of year when they need to be done.

So there you have it—from Total Mess to Total Rest. This is a flexible system that works for any home situation. Women all over the country have found it works, and have found ways to improve it. Susan Wetzel from Austin, Texas, wrote me this letter:

I prayed that there would be creative ways the Lord would show me to use the storage boxes. . . . Then as I passed by my telephone directories piled near the phone, an idea popped into my head. I stood a box on its "back" so that the lid opens down in front, and stacked the directories, yellow pages, and church directory in it like a bookcase. This way they are within easy reach and out of sight as well.

Susan McMaster from Van Nuys, California, went through the total-mess-to-total-rest process with her fiance. "It took the two of us every spare minute we could get for three straight weeks, but we did it!" she wrote. "I now know where everything is and in what box, just by taking a few minutes to go through my card file."

Martha McCutcheon in Bellaire, Michigan, put her card file in a repainted kid's lunch box, "So I can carry it from one living environment to another."

Diane from Upland, California, wrote: "I'm on Box 65 and still counting. I've given four huge trash bags full of stuff to the Salvation Army and that was after I cleaned the garage last year and gave them ten bags."

Now let me throw in one more idea.

The Children's File Box

When our children were about 12 years old, I set up a file box for each one of them. (I wish I had started this even earlier.) I gave each child ten folders and one day we went through the total-mess-to-total-rest program in their rooms. After we had organized all of their possessions, they began to file their report cards, special reports, pictures, letters, and other mementos. Jenny saved some love letters she had received. And when she bought her first car, her insurance papers went into the file box.

When the children went away to college, each of

them took his or her file box. When they returned home for the summer, their file boxes came home with them. When Jenny and Craig were married, she took her file box, loaded with memories and personal treasures, and began another file box for her new home. Now she keeps all her warranties, instruction booklets, insurance and other papers in one box. So this process can be a great teaching tool for your children.

Now that we have gone from total-mess-to-total-rest, what have we got? More Hours in Our Day! And no guilt feelings about an unorganized house. We have laid an important foundation. From here, let's go on to talk about some of the other stress-producing areas of our lives and see how we can also overcome them. Such as one of our most time-consuming activities—meal planning.

Chapter 6

Saving Time and Money by Meal Planning

> *"She is energetic, a hard worker, and watches for bargains. She works far into the night!"*
>
> Proverbs 31:17,18 TLB

The average homemaker plans, shops, chops, pares, cooks, and cleans up for more than 750 meals a year.

Feeding our families is certainly a major part of our lives. For the working woman, it can be a monumental task, especially if we are concerned about the nutritional content of our family's meals. Even the woman who's a full-time wife and mother can find this area an exhausting ordeal.

A few years ago, I found myself often serving as a short-order cook, trying to please everyone in the family. At any one breakfast I might fix French toast, waffles, scrambled eggs, pancakes, bacon, sausage, fruit, cold cereal, and oatmeal. By the time breakfast was over, I was ready to climb back into bed! I had to find a solution before I lost my sanity.

My solution was to plan a week's worth of breakfasts, incorporating each family member's favorite breakfast one morning each week. For example, on

Monday I might fix Brad's favorite, French toast; on Tuesday, Bob's favorite, fried eggs over medium; Wednesday, Jenny's favorite, waffles; and so on. I kept Sunday open for the cook's choice, or let my husband cook that morning.

It became such a pleasure to fix breakfast with this plan that I very quickly expanded my planning to all our meals. And it motivated me to begin looking for new and interesting recipes and to scour the newspapers for money-saving sales. Now I always plan my meals an entire week ahead, check my cupboards and pantry to see what I have on hand, and make a marketing list for my trip to the grocery store. It saves me time and money.

As I have shared these ideas with women at More Hours in My Day seminars, they find this system works. Women tell me that they have saved up to $12 per week by preplanning their meals. Hazel Acorn from Jamestown, New York, wrote to tell me that she had taken the idea and adapted a monthly menu plan:

> I planned a month's menu, along with a one-month shopping list. I have photocopied it and have used it for three months now, just shopping once a month. I now am revising my menu selections for the summer months, but I cannot tell you what a freedom this has given me not to have to clutter my mind with the details of shopping and considering what's for dinner.

Menu planning is especially helpful for working women. If it's 4:00 P.M. at work, she can wonder, "Did I take something out of the freezer? Do I have to stop by the store on my way home?" Or she can eliminate that hassle and anticipate going home, knowing she's planned dinner and has all the ingredients ready to go.

This is a flexible plan. If you schedule tuna casserole on Tuesday and find you don't feel like it that night, just switch meals. You have got all you need for the alternative. Or if you decide to eat out on "meat-loaf Thursday," simply move meat loaf over to next week. You have now got one meal planned for next week and everything you need to prepare it already in the house.

Let's see how the process works. In Exhibit P you can see a weekly menu chart filled out. Let's examine how we can prepare to shop, get the most for our money, prepare the food in the least amount of time, and have fun doing it.

Turning Coupons Into Cash

This is a great place to start as we plan our shopping list. Many smart women are saving money by couponing. I have found a 9" x 5½" accordion file is a great tool for organizing coupons. Topics for different sections might include:

- Personal/Health
- Soups
- Frozen
- Poultry/Meats
- Rice
- Baking products
- Baby
- Paper products
- Dry goods
- Breads
- Jams/Jellies
- Cookies
- Charcoal/Lighter
- Miscellaneous
- Mixes
- Laundry
- Sauces
- Cleaners
- Cereals
- Lunch meats
- Soda pop
- Dairy
- Package mixes
- Snacks
- Garden
- Coffee/Tea
- Salad/Seasonings

One important tip when cutting out coupons: Run a yellow highlighter pen over the expiration date. That way your eye will catch the date quickly. Periodically,

WEEKLY MENUS

DATE _May 5_

DAY OF WEEK	BREAKFAST	LUNCH	DINNER
MONDAY	7 grain cereal	Sack lunch	Mexican Mountains, salsa, dip
TUESDAY	Pancakes w/Turkey Patties		Baked Chicken, Baked Potatoes
WEDNESDAY	Scrambled eggs w/wheat toast		Halibut w/vegetables
THURSDAY	Belgian Waffles w/strawberries		Stir fry w/noodles
FRIDAY	Oatmeal w/rye toast		Italian Pasta Salad
SATURDAY	Eat Out at Coco's	Turkey w/cheese Sandwiches	Bar-B-Q Chicken, beans, biscuits
SUNDAY	Bran Muffins, Melons	Meat Loaf, Potatoes, Gravy	Soup, Salad, Crackers

go through your files and discard those coupons which have expired.

Some women save an amazing amount of money with coupons. I met one young mother who said she had saved $850 in one year by couponing. Another working woman saved $1,100. I asked them to share with me some of their ideas that allowed them to save that kind of money. Here are some of their suggestions:

• Use double-discount coupons whenever possible. These are store coupons in the local paper that double the value of any coupon. If your store does not use double coupons, it might be worth driving to another market that does. Used on items that are already on sale, you can save a lot of money. Suppose a store advertises coffee at a special $1.99 price. You have a 50 cents coupon for that brand of coffee. The store also has a double-discount coupon, so you can purchase a can of coffee for only 99 cents.

• Save coupons for "luxury" items (freezer bags, disposable diapers, pie crust mix, etc.) and keep an eye out for these things on a clearance table. They might be slightly damaged or a brand that's being discontinued by the store. With your coupon doubled, you might purchase it at a minimal price, or even for free. I bought a special mix for rye bread, clearance priced at 90 cents; with a 40 cents coupon doubled, the mix only cost me ten cents.

• On costly items, I will drive to another market for a great deal and stock up. For example, since we eat a lot of chicken, I'll look for a sale on chicken, and with my coupons and double coupons, buy up as much as my freezer and budget can handle.

• Couponing allows you to try new brands. You may find a better product in the sampling. But do this wisely. Ask yourself if you would have bought the item if there had been no coupon. And compare prices with competing brands to see if you are really saving money.

• Generic is *not* always the best buy. Often you can get a superior product for the same price or less by using a coupon.

• Never throw away a newspaper before you have clipped the coupons, even if you get more than one food section. Recently, my market doubled *all* other markets' coupons, so I made sure to check all the other store advertising sections for their coupons.

• Quickly check all junk mail and clip the coupons before you toss. Also magazines are a great source of coupons.

• Inform friends and relatives if you are looking for particular coupons. They may be willing to pass their unused coupons to you.

• Refunding may be complicated because most markets do not stock refund forms. My rule is that I don't buy these products unless I have the refund form (clipped from a magazine or newspaper). And I try to purchase those items when they are on sale, or with a doubled coupon, or best—both! And it must be something I use often, not a new, untested product. (Who wants three boxes of a terrible-tasting cereal taking up space in the cupboards?) I have found that many refunds are for combinations of foods I do not normally buy or use. And if the refund is for less than one dollar, it's not worth my effort. I find I save more by investing my energies in couponing.

And what do you do with the money you save? One woman told me that she writes her check for the total amount of the purchase before the checkout clerk subtracts her coupons. Then she pockets her savings and uses the money to purchase Christmas presents. Now that's one way to reduce the financial pressure of the holiday season!

Saving Money at the Supermarket

The best way to save money when you go shopping is to plan ahead. Your weekly menu is the crucial element in your planning. Here are some tips to keep in mind when planning your menu and making your shopping list.

Seasonal produce is usually your best buy. Green beans in season cost less per serving than canned or frozen, and provide better nutritional value.

Check your local newspaper ads for sales, especially at the meat counter. Stock up when possible. If tuna is on special, you might buy a dozen cans. They can be stored indefinitely. (More about stocking your pantry in the next chapter.) Eggs stored in their cartons will last four or five weeks. Many markets now specialize in bulk purchases. However, be cautious that you don't buy more than you need; spoilage can eliminate any savings you might have gained. Sharing with a neighbor or relative might make bulk buying more advantageous.

Generic brands are a great way to save money on certain items. Why purchase a top brand of stewed tomatoes when a generic brand will do great in that pot of chili? Generic brand napkins, paper towels, and toilet paper often provide a good savings.

Try not to do your grocery shopping on weekends. Most large markets up their prices on weekends, then lower them again on Monday, Tuesday, and Wednesday.

You might like to make a shopping list like the one shown in Exhibit Q. With this list, it only takes a few minutes to prepare my shopping list each week. (Exhibit Q shows a completed list, based on the sample menu.)

Now here are a few tips to keep in mind as you go to the supermarket:

SHOPPING LIST

DATE MAY 5

	Qty.	Cost

STAPLES

	Qty.	Cost
Cereal	___	___
Flour	___	___
Jello	___	___
Mixes	___	___
Nuts	___	___
Stuffing	___	___
Sugar	___	___

SPICES

	Qty.	Cost
Bacon Bits	___	___
Bak. Powder	___	___
Chocolate	___	___
Coconut	___	___
Salt/Pepper	✔	___
Soda	___	___

PASTA

	Qty.	Cost
Inst. Potato	___	___
Mixes	___	___
Pasta	✔	___
Rice	___	___
Spaghetti	✔	___

DRINKS

	Qty.	Cost
Apple Cider	✔	___
Coffee	___	___
Juice	✔	___
Sparkling	✔	___
Tea	___	___

CANNED GOODS

	Qty.	Cost
Canned Fruit	___	___
Strawberry	(1)	___
	___	___
	___	___
	___	___
Canned Meals	___	___
Canned Meat	___	___
Canned Vegetables	___	___
	___	___
	___	___
Soups		
Chicken	1	___
	___	___
Tuna	3	___

CONDIMENTS

	Qty.	Cost
Catsup	1	___
Honey	___	___
Jelly/Jam	✔	___
Mayonnaise	___	___
Molasses	___	___
Mustard	___	___
Oil	___	___
Peanut Butter	✔	___
Pickles	___	___
Relish	___	___
Salad Dressing	✔	___
Shortening	___	___
Syrup	___	___
Tomato Paste	___	___
Tomato Sauce	___	___
Vinegar	___	___

PAPER GOODS

	Qty.	Cost
Foil	___	___
Napkins	___	___
Paper Towels	___	___
Plastic Wrap	✔	___
Tissues	___	___
Toilet Paper	___	___
Toothpicks	___	___
Trash Bags	___	___
Waxed Paper	___	___
Zip Bags		
Small	___	___
Large	✔	___

HOUSEHOLD

	Qty.	Cost
Bleach	___	___
Clothes Soap	___	___
Dish Soap	___	___
Dishwasher Soap	___	___
Fab. Softener	✔	___
Furn. Polish	___	___
Light Bulbs	___	___
Pet Food	___	___
Vacuum Bags	___	___

FRESH PRODUCE

	Qty.	Cost
Fruit Apple	6	___
Oranges	6	___
banana	4	___
Vegetables		
Celery	1	___
lettuce	1	___

PERSONAL ITEMS

	Qty.	Cost
Body Soap	___	___
Deodorant	1	___
Fem. Protection	___	___
Hair Care	___	___
Make Up	___	___
	___	___
	___	___

FROZEN FOOD/JUICE

	Qty.	Cost
Ice Cream	___	___
	___	___
Juice		
Orange	✔	___
Pineapple	✔	___
T.V. Dinners	___	___
	___	___
Vegetables	___	___
	___	___
	___	___
	___	___

PASTRY

	Qty.	Cost
Bread/s	2	___
Buns	___	___
Chips	___	___
Cookies	___	___
Crackers	1	___
Croutons	___	___

MEAT

	Qty.	Cost
Beef	___	___
	___	___
Chicken	3	___
	___	___

DAIRY

	Qty.	Cost
Butter	1	___
Cheese	1#	___
Cottage Ch	1	___
Eggs	12	___
Milk	1Q	___
Sour Cream	___	___

EXHIBIT Q

1. *Avoid impulse buying.* Studies have estimated that nearly 50 percent of all purchases are unplanned. The purpose of having a shopping list is to help minimize impulse purchases that can destroy our budget and cause added stress. There are two times when we are most susceptible to temptation—at the start when our cart is nearly empty, and if we have to double back because we forgot an item on the list.

2. *Complete your shopping within half an hour.* You can do this by arranging your shopping list according to your store's floor plan. Supermarkets are often very comfortable places in which to linger. But that lingering can cause us to purchase items we really don't need. It's also best not to shop at "rush hour." At this time we have a greater tendency to pull items off the shelves without comparing prices.

3. *Shop alone if possible.* Children and husbands can cause us to compromise from our lists. Television advertising can cause kids to pressure us to buy the latest cereal, even though it is loaded with sugar and has little nutritional value.

4. *Never shop when hungry.* Enough said; the psychology is obvious.

5. *Understand supermarket psychology.* For instance, grocery stores stock their highest-priced items at eye level. Lower-priced staples like flour, sugar, and salt are often near the floor, as are bulk quantities of many items. Always check top and bottom shelves for similar items with lower price tags. Also, foods displayed at the end of aisles may appear to be on sale, but often they are not.

6. *Use unit pricing.* Many stores now do this for you. On the shelf tags, along with the price of an item, will be a number telling you the price of that item per pound or per cup. You can compare different brands and different sizes to see which is the best buy. Or purchase a pocket calculator and take it with you to the market

to figure the unit cost yourself. You can also use the calculator to keep a running total of your purchases, to help you stay within budget.

7. *Avoid foods packaged as individual servings.* Extra packaging usually boosts the price. A single family unit or a couple without children might be able to buy this way for convenience. But this is not an economical way to purchase food for families with children.

8. *Compare meat prices.* Notice the difference in the price per pound of boneless chicken breasts compared to whole chicken breasts with ribs. The filets often cost twice as much. You can filet chicken yourself by par boiling for 10 to 12 minutes and peeling the meat off the bone. But cheaper is not always better. Sometimes a relatively high-priced cut of beef with little or no waste may provide more meat for the money than a lower-priced cut with much bone, gristle, or fat. Chicken, turkey, and fish are often bargains for the budget buyer.

9. *Buy produce in season.* Never buy the first crop; prices are sure to go down. Fruits and vegetables purchased at the height of the season are at their peak quality and lowest price. Consider having an old-fashioned canning weekend to take advantage of your favorite produce, so you can enjoy them throughout the year.

10. *Study the labels.* As an informed consumer, you need to be aware of what the labels on your products mean. Manufacturers use additives and preservatives to give color and longer shelf life to their products. You may not be willing to make that trade-off.

What Food Labels Tell You

• INGREDIENTS. Ingredients must be listed in descending order of prominence by weight. So the first ingredients listed are the main ingredients in that product.

• COLORS AND FLAVORS. Added colors and flavors do not have to be listed by name. But the use of artificial colors or flavors must be indicated.

• SERVING CONTENT. Information must include the serving size; the number of calories per serving; the amount of protein, carbohydrates, and fat in each serving; the percentage of U.S. recommended daily allowance (U.S. RDA) for protein and seven important vitamins and minerals.

• OPTIONAL INFORMATION. Some labels also contain the following: the percentage of U.S. RDA for any of the 12 additional vitamins and minerals, the amount of saturated and unsaturated fat and cholesterol per serving, and the amount of sodium per serving.

What Food Labels Don't Tell You

• WHAT STANDARDIZED FOODS CONTAIN. More than 350 foods, including such common items as enriched white bread and catsup, are classified as "standardized." The FDA has established guidelines for these items and manufacturers are not required to list the ingredients.

• THE AMOUNT OF SUGAR IN SOME PRODUCTS. Sugar and sweeteners come in a variety of forms— white sugar, brown sugar, corn syrup, dextrose, sucrose, maltose, corn sweeteners—and if they're all listed separately, it's nearly impossible to know the actual amount of sugar contained in a labeled product.

• HOW "NATURAL" A PRODUCT IS. FDA guidelines for use of the word "natural" are loose. A "natural" product may, in fact, be highly processed and full of additives.

• SPECIFIC INGREDIENTS THAT MAY BE HARMFUL. Since coloring or spices that don't have to be listed by name can cause some people nausea, dizziness, or hives, it may be difficult to know exactly which products to avoid.

Saving Time Back at Home

Now that we've planned our menu and purchased our food, let's see what we can do to streamline our food preparation.

One tremendous time-saver is to prepare our food as soon as we bring it home from the market. No, I don't mean cook it—just prepare it. If you already know how you will use your vegetables, they can be cleaned, cut or chopped, placed in baggies or Tupperware containers, and stored in the refrigerator—ready for salads, steamed vegetables, soups, or casseroles. Onions and green peppers can be chopped, placed in an airtight container or baggie, and frozen. A large block of cheese can be grated and frozen, allowing you to remove a portion whenever needed.

Salad greens can be cleaned, drained, and stored for the week's salads. An easy way to remove the water from greens is to put them in a lingerie bag (a mesh bag available at grocery and drug stores) and place them in your washing machine on "spin" cycle for about two minutes. That spins out all the water, and the greens will stay fresh and crisp for up to two weeks when stored in a baggie or plastic container in the refrigerator. (But don't leave your washing machine while the lettuce is spinning. One woman walked away and forgot about the lettuce and didn't discover it until three days later.)

Fruit prepared ahead of time will keep well if you squeeze lemon juice over it, toss, and refrigerate. The juice of half a lemon is enough for up to two quarts of cut fruit.

Now here are a few other ideas for saving time and money in your food preparation:

1. Turn your no-longer-fresh bread and crackers into crumbs for use in stuffings, casseroles, and meat loaf. Just put them in the blender, turn it on and count to three, then put the crumbs in a plastic bag for storage.
2. Save oil from deep frying. Strain through cheesecloth and keep refrigerated.
3. Citrus fruit yields more juice at room temperature.
4. Use the time when you're watching television for jobs like shelling nuts. Children often like to help in this task, especially if they can nibble while they help.
5. Learn to do two things at once when working in the kitchen. I highly recommend a long extension cord for your phone so it can reach every corner of the kitchen. While you're on the phone you can:

*   Load or unload the dishwasher
*   Clean the refrigerator
*   Cook a meal
*   Bake a cake
*   Mop the floor
*   Clean under the kitchen sink

No doubt you can come up with many other ways to do two things at once.

6. Practice this time-saving rule: **Don't put it down, put it away.** We spend many extra minutes handling an item two or three times. Discipline yourself to handle it once and put it directly away.
7. Take advantage of any convenience appliances you have, such as a microwave oven or food processor. They can be a costly luxury if they aren't used; but a wonderful time-saver for the busy mother and working woman.
8. Plan your timetable for meal preparation so the

cooked vegetables aren't done ten minutes before the chicken. Vegetables like green beans and broccoli can quickly lose color, texture, flavor, and nutritional value. Timing your meal preparation may take some trial and error, but with a little practice you will become very capable.

Debbie Thompson of Chino, California, wrote to me after attending one of my seminars. She has more ideas for saving time in the kitchen:

> I decided to try your suggestions of preparing everything I could right when I got home from the grocery store. I started with a few items and then looked at the clock and just kept going and got more and more excited. So I pulled out a piece of paper and wrote down the list.... We have never eaten so good for an entire week and my husband is no longer buying lunches out, which saves us more money. Here's what I did:
>
> 1. Boiled eggs for the week
> 2. Made a Jello salad
> 3. Washed, drained, and spun lettuce as you suggested
> 4. Cooked and cut turkey breast for lunches
> 5. Cut carrot and celery sticks, and zucchini, too
> 6. Made a dip
> 7. Packaged nutes and raisins for lunches
> 8. Put all other groceries away
> 9. Mixed the frozen juice for the week
> 10. Made a potato salad
> 11. Made tuna salad for sandwiches
> 12. Made orange juice popsicles for treats
> 13. Put chips and cookies for lunches in baggies
> 14. Made a meat loaf for tonight's dinner

15. Washed potatoes to bake for tonight's dinner

I had interruptions and it (still) only took me two hours. Not only did I save time, but money too. Plus it released my stress and frustration over meals and lunches.

Now that's organization! I've prepared a "Saving Time & Money Checklist" (Exhibit R shows one filled out) to help you chart your own progress. All you do is answer "yes" or "no" to each question at the end of a week. If the answer if "yes" to most of the questions, you are on your way to being more efficient and you will have more time and money for other activities. If you answer "no," evaluate how you can change your habit so it can become a "yes" next week. There's also space to add to the checklist. Do this for a few weeks until you can answer "yes" to every question. You'll find meal preparation will become a joy rather than a mental and physical hassle.

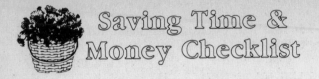

Saving Time & Money Checklist

Week Of: _____

OPPORTUNITIES TO SAVE	CHOICE YES	NO	CHANGE OF HABIT
1. Did I plan my menus this week?	✓		*So much easier.*
2. Did I work off a shopping list this week?	✓		*So much faster.*
3. Did I avoid extra trips to the market this week?	✓		*only one trip.*
4. Did I go to the market when I wasn't hungry?	✓		*snacky food was off.*
5. Did I have better timing with food preparation?		✓	*I still need to work on coming together.*
6. Did I take advantage of my microwave this week? My food processor?	✓ ✓		
7. Did I save costs by purchasing seasonal fruits? Vegetables?	✓ ✓		*Fresh Pears. Fresh Corn.*

OPPORTUNITIES TO SAVE	CHOICE YES	NO	CHANGE OF HABIT
8. When shopping, did I do price comparison before selecting an item?	✓		I even switched on a couple of brands.
9. Did I check local newspaper for special ads and coupons?	✓		Saved $4.00 last week.
10. Did I avoid impulse purchases?	✓		No shopping at the cash register.
11. Did I stay within my budget?	✓		I was $8.00 below budget.
12. Did I look for bulk packaging to save?	✓		Beans.
13. Was I able to save money by purchasing day-old bread and rolls?	✓		4 rolls at 1/2 price.
14. Was I able to save money by using more chicken and turkey in my menus?		✓	Not this week, but next week.
15. Did I avoid shopping on the weekend? Busy time of day?	✓ ✓		The traffic jam wasn't there.

OPPORTUNITIES TO SAVE	CHOICE YES	NO	CHANGE OF HABIT
16. Did I purchase a generic brand item this week?	✓		The stewed tomatoes were great.
17. Did I shop out of a catalog this week?	✓		Ordered several items from L.L. Bean
18. Did I reorganize at least one item in my kitchen this week to make it more convenient?	✓		Rearranged spices in A-B-C order.
19. Did I prepare some foods when I came home from the market to save me time later?	✓		Washed lettuce. grated cheese. Chopped nuts.
20. Did I save time in food preparation while watching TV?	✓		Snapped green beans. Cracked nuts.
21. Was I able to apply the rule, "Don't put it down, put it away!" this week?	✓		It reduced the clutter.

OPPORTUNITIES TO SAVE	CHOICE		CHANGE OF HABIT
	YES	NO	
22. Did I eliminate extra steps by pre-planning my activities?	✓		*I planned the cleaners, nursery, around marketing.*
23. Other _____ _____ _____ _____		✓	

Chapter 7

Planning an Efficient Pantry and Kitchen

*E*very woman should have a pantry. It's an essential element in organizing our meals, saving money, and relieving much of the stress today's women experience. Unfortunately many women do not have a separate room they can devote to a pantry. But you can make a pantry out of one section of the kitchen cupboards. Or put some cupboards in a nearby area such as the laundry room, mud room, or garage. Preferably, your freezer should be located here. And if you have a large family, you might have an extra refrigerator, too. (It can be an old unit, or if you buy a new refrigerator, keep the old one for your pantry.) Your pantry will become a storehouse of confidence right at your fingertips.

If you are starting a pantry, or rethinking your pantry area, use this time to clean off the shelves with a good household cleaning solution. It will give the pantry an extra hygienic smell. You might even buy some cheerful new shelf paper to give the area brightness. Several lazy Susans are great for providing added shelf space and make it easier to reach certain items without knocking over bottles and cans.

I suggest that a pantry contain a supply of basic staple foods, including starches, sweets, condiments, canned or bottled items, and perishable goods. Most of the dry items that have a long shelf life, such as pasta, beans, and rice, can be purchased in bulk when they are on sale. Other items such as perishable foods may have to be replenished on your weekly trip to the grocery store.

Here are some elements that should be in every pantry:

Starches

- Flour
- Cornmeal
- Boxed cereal
- Pasta
- White or brown rice
- Oatmeal
- A variety of potatoes (Red potatoes are especially versatile. They're good boiled, roasted, fried, or in potato salad, and require a minimum of cooking time.)

These items can be used as a staple for any entree, as a side dish, or as a hearty addition to soups and stews.

Sweet-based Staples

- Honey
- Brown and white sugar
- Apple juice
- Maple syrup
- Jams and jellies

Condiments

- Catsup
- Brown and/or yellow mustard

- Vinegar
- Pickles
- Capers
- Worchestershire sauce
- Oil
- Olives
- Salsa
- Canned tuna or any other canned fish or meat. These can be stocked for easy sandwiches, salads, dips, casseroles, and omelets.

Dried or Canned Fruits and Vegetables

- Green beans
- Fruit cocktail
- Raisins
- Variety of soups
- Tomatoes
- Apple sauce
- Prunes

Perishable Foods (if you have an extra refrigerator)

- Celery
- Green peppers
- Tomatoes
- Eggs
- Nuts
- Garlic (a great source of flavor)
- Onions (green, yellow, and white)
- Lemons
- Cheese (yellow and white)
- Frozen juices

From breakfast to dessert, you will find all of these items welcome helpers in meal preparation.

Here are a few helpful hints for making the most of your pantry:

1. When stocking your pantry, organize your staples and canned goods in categories such as canned fruit, canned vegetables, meats, juices, cereals, etc.

2. Keep an inventory of your pantry (See Exhibit S). Plan your menus using this list and shop only once a week, replenishing staples as necessary. Restock *before* you run out to avoid those "emergency" trips to the market when unexpected company arrives.

3. Leave enough room in your freezer and storage space to take advantage of sales and coupons so you can stock up and save money.

4. Place a colored dot on items you've purchased for a future recipe to warn your husband and children that these are not to be used for snacks.

5. Have a "cooking marathon." This could be fun to do as a family or with a special friend. Prepare several entrees, breads, cakes, cookies, casseroles, spaghetti sauce, or soups. Freeze them in family-size portions (plus a few individual servings), making sure they're labeled and dated. Or try doubling the recipe whenever you cook a favorite soup or casserole. Feed half to the family and the other half to the freezer for later use.

6. Make your own TV dinners by using a sectional paper plate or pie tin and add leftovers to each section. These will provide great dinners after an especially busy day, or when Mom's away.

7. Investigate using a food service. It allows you to save time and money by shopping on the phone and ordering meats and staples for six months at a time. They deliver right to your house, and often put the groceries away for you. This way your weekly shopping is limited to perishables, and often you can zip through the express line at the checkout counter.

Now let's continue to one of the most challenging activities in every woman's home—organizing the kitchen.

PANTRY INVENTORY LIST

STORAGE ITEM	QUANTITY ON HAND	NEED TO PURCHASE	COMMENTS
☐ Basic Cookbook	1	1	Update
☐ Storage Containers			
Baggies	2	2 baggies	
Jars	8		
Plastic	1	tupperware	Go to neighborhood party
☐ Wheat Flour	8 #	—	
☐ White Flour	2 #	—	
☐ Nonfat Dried Milk	1	1 box	
☐ Sugar/Honey	OK	—	
☐ Salt/Pepper	OK	—	
☐ Yeast	1	—	
☐ Baking Soda	1½ box	—	
☐ Baking Powder	1 can	1	
☐ Shortening	1	1	
☐ Oil	1	1	
☐ Peanut Butter	1	1	
☐ Canned/Dried Vegetables			
carrot		2 bags	
celery			
☐ Variety of Dried Legumes			
Kidney Beans	2 #	1 #	
Pinto Beans	2 #	1 #	
Navy Beans	1 #	2 #	purchase
Soybeans	1 #	2 #	bulk
Lentils	2 #	1 #	
Peas	3 #	—	
☐ Variety of Grains			
Rice	—	2 #	
Oats	—	2 #	
Rye	—	2 #	
Barley	—	2 #	
☐ Corn	5 cans	—	
☐ Canned/Dried Fruit			
Peaches	—	2 #	dried
Prunes	—	2 #	✓
Raisins	—	2 #	✓
Strawberries	—	3 cartons	frozen
☐ Canned Sauces			
tomato	1	1	
clam	1	1	
Hollandaise	1	1	
☐ Canned Meats			
tuna	1	3	
chicken	1	3	
spam	1	—	

PANTRY INVENTORY LIST

STORAGE ITEM	QUANTITY ON HAND	NEED TO PURCHASE	COMMENTS
☐ Margarine/Butter	2#	—	
☐ Soup	3 cans	6 cans	assorted
☐ Vinegar	—	1	
☐ Vanilla	1 bottle	—	
☐ Vitamin C	2 bottles	—	
☐ Bouillon Cubes	2 cartons	—	
☐ Chocolate/Carob	1 carton	—	
☐ Canned Milk	1	3	
☐ Pastas			
Lasagna	1	1	
Macaroni	1	1	
Rotelli	1	1	
Spaghetti	1	2	
☐ Salad Dressing	2 bottles		
☐ Cornmeal	3 boxes	—	
☐ Raisins	O K		
☐ Gelatin	1 box		
☐ Pickles/Olives	1 Jar		
☐ Catsup	1 bottle	1 bottle	
☐ Herbs/Spices			
Oregano	—	1	
Thyme	—	1	
Sage	1	—	
Basil	1	—	
☐ Soy Sauce	O K	—	
☐ Worcestershire Sauce	O K	—	
☐ Dried Onion	1½ bottle	—	
☐ Garlic	O K		
☐ Coffee/Tea	1#	3#	Decaffinated
☐ Herb Teas	—	2 boxes	water/process
☐ Wheat Grinder	—	—	investigated—
☐ Other			will purchase for june.

Planning the Kitchen

Many women envy a well-planned kitchen, viewing their own as an obstacle course to efficient cooking. No matter how large or small, any kitchen can be tailored to suit your style, if you will give some thought to your cooking habits and needs.

Let's start by taking inventory of your kitchen. These are what I consider the essentials:

Pans

- One 10'' skillet with lid
- One 8'' to 10'' omelet pan
- A set of covered casserole dishes
- 1 roasting pan with rack
- 2 bread pans
- 2 cookie sheets
- 1 double boiler
- 1 dutch oven or similar type of pan

Basic Utensils

Good utensils start with the knives. It took Bob and me 30 years before we finally invested in a good set of knives. Now I wish I'd done it years ago. Included with the set should be a steel sharpener to keep your knives properly maintained.

Other necessary utensils include:

- 1 set of measuring cups
- A variety of wooden spoons
- 1 mallet (for tenderizing less expensive cuts of meat)
- 1 spatula
- Shears (great for cutting parsley, green onions, and meat)

- 1 rolling pin
- Storage bowls
- 1 vegetable cleaner
- 1 cheese slicer
- Tongs
- 1 garlic press (I use this often)

Gadgets

- Grater
- Colander
- Sifter
- Vegetable steamer
- Food grinder
- Egg beater
- Wisk
- Egg slicer

Optional Larger Equipment

These items are long-range money and time-saving investments:

- Mixer
- Toaster oven
- Blender
- Food processor
- Wheat mill
- Microwave oven (A very large gadget!)
- Freezer

The key rule in organizing your kitchen is, "Things that work together are stored together." Take a few minutes to think through your daily work pattern and plan your space accordingly. For example, if you do a lot of baking, set up a baking center. It might be a counter top or a convenient cupboard or even a mobile worktable that can be rolled into your kitchen on baking day. Your mixer, baking pans, utensils, and cannisters should all be readily accessible to this center.

Items seldom used, such as a turkey platter, deviled egg dish, roasting pan, seasonal tableware, and picnic gear, should be kept on higher shelves or stored in the garage on a special, easily accessible shelf. That will free space in your kitchen for the regularly-used items.

Here are three other ideas for your kitchen:

1. Spices can be found quickly if stored in alphabetical order on a lazy Susan or a wooden spice rack on your wall.

2. Use a crock to store utensils such as wooden spoons, wisks, meat mallet, ladles, and spatula on the stove. This can free up a drawer and allows for quick retrieval.

3. If you get a new set of flatware, keep the old set for parties, to loan out when friends have buffets or church socials, or for family camping trips.

Once you've planned and organized your pantry and kitchen, you'll be amazed how much time you save and how much smoother mealtime preparation goes. Look for new and more efficient ways to store your equipment and food. Study the kitchen and gourmet sections of your department stores for ideas and tools that can save you even more time.

Chapter *8*

What to Do with All the Paper

Most of us can't wait for the mail to arrive each day. We eagerly anticipate a letter from a special relative or friend, or grab for our favorite magazine. At the same time, the thought of processing numerous bills, solicitations, and other mailings can be depressing. What do we save? Where do we put the things hubby needs to read—if and when he gets around to it? And what do we throw away?

Every day we must make decisions about paper—from mail to children's art projects, to church bulletins and notices, to newspapers and magazines—and much, much more. It seems like we must sort through mountains of papers that accumulate from day to day, week to week, month to month. How can we ever conquer this problem and control our paper, rather than allowing it to bury us?

One woman solved her problem by hiring a person to help organize all her accumulated papers. As a school teacher, she had acquired and saved volumes of research, teaching ideas, school notices, and student reports. Together the pair worked three hours a day, five days a week, for three months during summer vacation—a total of 180 hours each. But the teacher's problem still wasn't solved, because she needed to develop a system for dealing with paper at the moment it arrived.

Sometimes it takes a major crisis to motivate us to attack the paper problem. One lady couldn't use her dining room table without a major paper transfer. That happened only when she entertained company. Another woman's husband, fed up with piles stacked on counters, refrigerator, desk, game table, dressers, and even the floor, threatened, "Either the papers go or I go." That ultimatum caused her to bring her paper epidemic under control.

Paper organization usually isn't a problem early in our single or married life. A few insurance policies, the apartment rental agreement, marriage license, diploma, and checking account statements and cancelled checks, lure us into thinking a full-fledged filing system isn't necessary. All the important papers fit comfortably in a shoebox or metal fireproof box that is stored on a closet shelf.

But as the years go by, we collect appliance warranties, instruction booklets, "his" graduate school records, "her" real estate license papers, baby's birth certificate and first picture, not to mention the countless receipts for IRS tax purposes. The result is paper chaos. We dare not throw anything away for fear of accidently tossing something important. We might set up an accordion file or put a few file folders in a drawer in a kitchen desk, but many of the papers are stacked, waiting for that "rainy day" when we'll sort them. When we have to locate an important item, it's a frantic scramble. How we wish we'd gotten organized a long time ago.

Don't despair. Help is on the way. There is one rule and six basic steps for effective paper management.

The rule: **Don't put it down; put it away.**

Most of our frustration with paper can be avoided if we deal with it the first time. Unfortunately, most of us aren't there. So let's see how we can organize so we never have to be buried under the paper mountain again.

1. Schedule time to sort through papers. Put it on your daily schedule. Make it a part of the index cards in the weekly section of your card file. If you don't schedule it, you won't do it.

2. Assemble some materials to help you get organized:

- Metal file cabinet or file boxes
- Plastic trash bags (the 30-gallon size work great)
- File folders (I prefer brightly colored folders, but plain manila will do)
- Plain white #10 envelopes (or larger, if needed)
- Black felt-tip marking pen

3. Begin. Start wherever the clutter annoys you most. Determine to work your way through every pile of paper. Go through drawers and closets where paper has accumulated. Continue at set times until the project is completed. (You may want to make this part of the Total-Mess-to-Total-Rest project we outlined in Chapter 5, allotting a minimum of 15 minutes per day for a few days or weeks.)

4. Determine to throw away anything you don't need.

- Perhaps you have a lot of articles, recipes, or children's school papers and art work. *In each category, choose five pieces and toss the rest into your trash bag.*

• Don't get bogged down. Rereading old love letters, recipes, or articles divert you from your purpose of organizing the papers.

• You don't need to keep receipts of clothing you bought several years ago.

• If you're having trouble making decisions, ask a friend to help. She can be objective. Later, you can return the favor when she decides to attack *her* paper piles.

• Keep legal papers and tax records for a minimum of seven years. If you operate a business, you need to keep all papers, sales ledgers, inventory records, cancelled checks, and bank statements in case an audit is required.

5. Develop a simple yet thorough file system.

• Label file folders with a felt pen. Files might include:

Bible study notes/ outlines	Mortgage
IRS tax information for (year)	Photos/negatives
Bank statements/cancelled checks	Home improvement receipts
Charge accounts	Vacation ideas
Utility receipts	Christmas card lists
Investment records	Home improvement ideas
Insurance policies	Restaurants
Insurance claims	Warranties
Car repair receipts	Instruction booklets
Charitable giving records	

• Label a file folder for each member of the family. These files can be used to keep health records, report cards, notes, drawings, awards, and other special remembrances.

• Within each file, use plain envelopes to separate accounts. For example, in the "Utility Receipts" folder, there might be separate envelopes labeled:

GAS	ELECTRICITY
OIL	WATER/SEWER
TELEPHONE	GARBAGE COL- LECTION

• When necessary, add files so no one file is too thick. For instance, instead of one insurance file, there might be separate files for house, car, health, and life insurance policies.

• *Handle each piece of paper once.* Decide where to file it, or toss it in the trash bag.

6. Store your files in an out-of-sight, yet easily-accessible place. If you're fortunate to have space in your home for a small office, then use a small file cabinet or desk file drawer for current files. The rest can be stored in a closet, garage, or attic. Make sure boxes are clearly marked by number and have a corresponding 3" x 5" card in the storage section of your card file (see Chapter 5 for more details). If a box contains crucial records that might need to be removed in an emergency such as a fire, put a bright red dot on the box so it can be easily recognized.

Staying on Top of Paper

Several women have asked me about buying a home computer to help them get organized. I do not believe a computer will solve the paper problem. The solution is to tackle the mountain of papers as we've described.

Then as new paper comes into your home, deal with it right away, filing or tossing each piece. You should have a place to store your bills until they are paid. Once a bill is paid, file the receipt immediately.

Managing the Mail

Now, let's talk about the mail. The key to managing this area of our lives is doing it daily. If it can't be done when it arrives, assign a time sometime that day to process it. One area of your home should be designated for this purpose—a desk, table, a section of the kitchen counter. (However, if you use the kitchen counter, be careful it doesn't become a catchall area. One woman told me she put her mail on top of her refrigerator. It piled so high that it took her three weeks to go through it.)

Remember our rule about paper: **Don't put it down; put it away.** It only takes a minute to sort the mail when it arrives, even if you can't process it at that moment. A simple file system can help you do this. One file could be for letters you want to read. If you have older children, each might have his or her folder to check when arriving home from school. Another file should be for your husband. There needs to be a file for bills, another for things you need to discuss with someone in the family, one for mail that needs to be answered, and perhaps another for those that require a phone call.

Many times people ask me questions by letter. If the person is someone I know, I usually prefer to call rather than write. It's quicker and many times a long-distance call is cheaper for me than writing a letter. (I try to take advantage of the cheapest rates when calling long distance.)

One woman told me she covered shoe boxes with wallpaper, labeled the boxes for various categories of mail, and set them in a row on a shelf. This allowed her to process her mail quickly. Remember, however, that with file folders or boxes, we still must beware of pileups. That's why I believe it's best to finalize action on each piece of mail within 24 hours. This way, mail never becomes a burden.

Here are a few other time-savers for mail processing:

• I consider junk mail a time-waster and toss it. It's tempting to think, "I may use this someday." The truth is that you most likely will not.

• For mail that requires input from another family member, I put a note or question mark on it so we can discuss it. Removable self-stick note pads are great for this.

• Sometimes I don't have time to read publications, missionary letters, and magazines. I slip them into a file folder and take them with me in the car. When I have to wait in a doctor's office or for the children, or even in a long line, I use that time to catch up on my mail reading. As I read, I may make notes on it, and when I'm done I toss it or process it according to its category.

• Address changes should be noted immediately upon receipt, making sure you cross out the old address in your address book to avoid confusion later.

• An R.S.V.P. should be answered as soon as you know your plans. This is a proper courtesy to your host or hostess and he or she will appreciate your promptness. If you can't give a quick "yes" or "no" answer, then let that be known, too.

• Make note on your calendar as soon as an invitation arrives. With our busy lives, we can't depend on our memories.

Mail and paper are a part of our daily lives. We can't make them disappear, but we can manage them. A little organization in this area can relieve a lot of stress.

Chapter 9

Washing and Caring for Our Clothes

"Create in me a clean heart, O God."

Psalm 51:10 KJV

It's Monday morning and the kids are madly dashing around, searching for matching socks. A matching pair is nowhere to be found and in frustration you inform your children that the washing machine has actually eaten their footwear.

Sound familiar? Like other areas of home management, our clothing and laundry can be organized in a way that will keep our socks in pairs, save precious time, and in the process teach our children organization techniques.

What about the sock problem? A simple way to solve it is to buy some inexpensive plastic sock sorts or safety pins and pair up your socks before putting them in the washer.

Another time-saver is to have three large bags for dirty clothes:

- A bright calico print bag for coloreds
- A white pillow case for whites

> • A navy denim bag for dark clothes such as
> jeans

Colored plastic trash cans also make good laundry sorters. Label the cans "colored," "white," and "dark."

The idea is to eliminate the time it takes to sort the clothing; it's already sorted for you. Show your family how to sort their own clothes by putting them in the proper bags or cans. Also announce to the family that whatever goes into the wash inside-out comes out the same way. It's up to them to make sure their clothes are right-side-out.

Now that your family's socks are paired and their clothes are sorted, you can concentrate on scheduling your wash days. Young mothers with one or more children in diapers may need to wash every day. For others, one to three times a week is enough. The important thing is to plan your laundry days ahead of time, and start early in the day. I realize that for working mothers this may not be possible. But leaving laundry for Saturday won't cut it either. What you may need to do is toss a load in the wash as soon as you arrive home from work. If your kids are older, delegate to them the job of transferring the wash to the dryer and sorting and folding the clothes when they're dry.

You might be tempted to start a load right before you leave for work. Resist that temptation. A machine leak or short circuit can cause damage, or worse, start a fire. So never leave the washer or dryer on when no one is home.

Here are a few tips on handling laundry:

> • Use cold water whenever possible. This is especially important with colored clothes; cold water helps the colors stay brighter longer.
> • Wash full loads rather than small loads. This saves energy plus wear and tear on your machines.

• Remove clothes from the dryer as soon as it stops. If you forget and a load sits for a while, simply throw in a damp towel and turn on the dryer for another ten minutes. The dampness from the towel will freshen the load and remove any set wrinkles.

• Hang as many clothes as possible, especially permanent press garments, on hangers. This will cut down on ironing. I recommend using plastic, colored hangers rather than metal. They prevent marks and creases. Put a few hooks in the laundry area to keep hangers handy, or string an indoor clothesline.

• Colored hangers can also be used to code your family's clothes. Assign each family member a different color and as you pull their clothing out of the dryer, hang them on the appropriate colored hangers.

• Consider color-coding underwear and socks by buying each family member his own color or pattern. If this isn't possible, try marking each person's underwear with embroidery thread or laundry pens.

• Color-coding also works well with folded clothes. Purchase a different colored bin (the size of a dishpan) for each member of the family, and store them on a shelf in your laundry area. As you fold the garments, sort them in the appropriate individual bins. It's up to each family member to empty the bin and put his or her own clothes away.

• Plan one day a week for ironing. (It should be an item in the weekly section of your card file.) One way to help pass the time is to pray for the one whose clothing you are ironing. This can make a normally mundane chore a real blessing and joy.

• Label your linen closet shelves so that whoever puts away the sheets and towels will know the right place for them. This saves time and confusion and keeps your closet looking neat.

It may take a little time and ingenuity to get your

laundry organized, but it's worth it. Just think what a relief it will be to see your children going off to school each day with matching socks!

So far, we've concentrated on managing the family's laundry needs. Now let's talk for a moment about our own clothing.

Personal Clothing Care

With the high cost of clothing and fabrics these days, we need to be aware of what we can do to keep our clothing looking fresh and new. Here are 20 ways to stretch the use of your wardrobe through proper care:

1. Dry clean garments only every eight to ten wearings; less frequently, if possible. Dry cleaning is hard on fabrics.

2. Rotate clothing so that it can regain its shape. A friend of mine rotates her garments by hanging them to the far right of her closet after each wearing. The next day she picks a blouse, pair of pants, or skirt on the left side of the closet. This way she knows how often they are worn. This also works well with the suits in men's closets.

3. As soon as you remove your garments, empty the pockets, shake the garments well, and hang them immediately.

4. Consider Scotchguarding new fabrics. The protection will last until the clothing is cleaned or washed. Then just spray again. Also, use Scotchguard on any of your fabric shoes.

5. Mend rips, loose hems, and loose buttons immediately. My husband has a tendency to tear out the seat of his pants, so I triple-stitch and zigzag the seams when they are new, even before they are worn. This keeps embarrassing moments to a minimum.

6. Keep from snagging your hose by using hand lotion to soften your hands before putting on nylons.

7. Hang wrinkled clothes in the bathroom while showering. The steam will cause wrinkles to fall out.

8. Let perfumes and deodorants dry on your body before dressing to prevent garment damage.

9. I put a scarf over my head before pulling on a garment to prevent a messed hairdo and makeup smudges and stains.

10. Hang blazers and coats on padded hangers to avoid hanger marks.

11. Store sweaters in a drawer or shelf rather than on a hanger to prevent stretching.

12. Skirts and pants are best hung on hangers with clips—or you can use clothespins on wire hangers.

13. Even good jewelry can discolor your clothing, so dab the back of it with clear nail polish. The polish can also be painted on jewelry with rough edges that may pull fibers of fabrics. (You probably shouldn't do this with real gold or silver as it will ruin the value of the jewelry.)

14. Some stick pins can run or make holes in delicate fabrics. Don't wear them if you are in doubt.

15. Be sure to keep your good leather shoes polished to retain shine and help preserve the leather.

16. Brush suede shoes with a suede brush that brings up the nap. You can use a nail file to rub off any little spots.

17. Replace heels and soles on your shoes before they wear down and cause damage.

18. If your shoes get wet, stuff them with paper towels or newspaper and allow them to dry away from heat.

19. Shoe trees are a great way to keep the shape in your shoes.

20. When storing leather handbags or shoes, never put them in plastic bags. That can cause the leather to

dry out. Use fabric shoe bags or wrap shoes in tissue and put them in shoe boxes.

And now a word about planning and maintaining your wardrobe. This is an important element for enhancing your professional and personal image. Remember, you rarely get a second chance to make a first impression. These three P's summarize my philosophy:

- Plan—your wardrobe
- Prepare—your look
- Present—yourself

Clean out your closet: Remove everything you don't wear, don't like, or don't feel good about wearing.

Inventory your clothes: Take a wardrobe inventory (see Exhibit T). As you review your inventory list, you can quickly see your overages (those clothes that are old and out-of-style) and shortages. Your overages are candidates for a future garage sale. Your shortage list helps you plan your shopping. With today's buying alternatives, you can find a wide range of quality and price in clothing. I prefer to purchase quality garments that will last longer, in order to maximize my dollar value.

Plan a wardrobe that works: Start with three basic items in a solid color and the same fabric: a blazer or jacket, a skirt, and pants. Then add blouses in solid or print colors to coordinate, and a couple of sweaters and accessories such as scarves, ribbon ties, belts, jewelry, and a silk flower or two. Select each item so it can mix and match with the three basic clothing items. For shoes, choose one casual pair and one dressy pair to complement your basics. With a little imagination and these six to nine items, you can create 20 outfits!

Each season, or whenever possible, add one new basic outfit to your wardrobe. If you have a trained

WARDROBE INVENTORY

BLOUSES	PANTS	SKIRTS

JACKETS	SWEATERS	DRESSES

GOWNS	LINGERIE	SHOES

JEWELRY	

THINGS I NEVER WEAR	THINGS I NEED

EXHIBIT T

professional color and wardrobe consultant in your area, you might want to consider investing in that service. It will save you time in shopping and you'll know that you're selecting the color and clothing style that makes you look your best.

Chapter 10

Sewing and Crafts Solutions

"She has no fear of winter for her household, for she has made warm clothes for all of them. She also upholsters with finest tapestry; her own clothing is beautifully made."

Proverbs 31:21,22 TLB

*T*oday's creative women find their closets, drawers, and bedrooms filled with the clutter of craft items, patterns, fabrics, straw flowers, glue guns, and fiberfill. It would be wonderful to have a room devoted exclusively to sewing and crafts. However, most of us must make do with a corner of the bedroom, living room, or even the garage. Piles of clutter can overwhelm us and the family. How can we organize all of this mess and retrieve any item quickly when needed? It's really very simple.

Here are the tools you need to solve the problem:

- Several "perfect boxes" for storage. Or if you prefer, use plastic bins, laundry baskets, plastic stacking trays, or wooden boxes.
- Several small jars (baby food style)
- 3" x 5" cards
- Pen
- Shoe boxes

If you've read the total-mess-to-total-rest chapter, you'll recognize some of the process. You can add boxes of craft and sewing items to your storage, listing them by number on 3" x 5" cards in the "Storage" section of your card file. This is a simple and fast way of retrieving items quickly.

Let's take your patterns. They can be organized and stored according to size and types—play clothes, dressy outfits, costumes, sport clothing, blouses, pants, etc. Many fabric stores carry cardboard boxes made specifically for storing patterns, and their cost is low.

The process is the same for fabrics. Put them in piles according to color: prints, solids, stripes, etc. Then place each pile in a separate cardboard perfect box, number the box, and fill out a corresponding 3" x 5" card. Your cards might look something like this:

Box 1—Calico fabrics
         Reds and pinks
Box 2—Solid fabrics
         Blues, browns, blacks
Box 3—Stripes, polka dots
Box 4—Remnants and scraps, a yard or less

Repeat the process with arts and craft items. Now for some more ideas for organizing all those buttons, pins, hooks, snaps. . . .

• Organize buttons on safety pins, pipe cleaners, or twist ties. Or stick loose bottons and snaps on strips of transparent tape.

• Store bias tape, piping, and hem tape in a shoe-box. Don't forget to clearly label the box.

• Store hook and eyes, snaps, and buttons in baby food jars. They will look so organized when lined on a shelf, or even when stored in shoe boxes (appropriately labeled, of course!).

• If you don't have a bobbin box, string bobbins on

pipe cleaners or keep them in a plastic ice cube tray or egg carton. This is also a great way to store safety pins, buttons, and other miscellaneous small items.

• To organize spools of thread, group them according to color and lay them on their sides in a drawer or in shoe box tops. Stack the box tops so that the most frequently used colors are on top.

• Discarded shoe boxes are great for storing sewing supplies and smaller arts and crafts items. Be sure you label the boxes so you know their contents.

• Fabric fill or stuffing and quilting materials can be stored in cardboard perfect boxes using the numbering system. So can straw and silk flowers and other such items.

• For craft projects, a hot glue gun is terrific. Be sure to unplug it when not in use and store it out of the reach of children. Let it cool before placing it in its storage area.

• Egg cartons are good organizers. The small compartments are great for pins, small craft items, paper clips, stamps, etc.

• Clamp pattern pieces together with a clothespin until you finish the project and return them to the envelope.

• Large manila envelopes are also great for organization and storage. The contents can be listed on the outside and stored in perfect boxes or a drawer. Items you might store this way are: fabric scraps, ribbons, pipe cleaners, lace, bias tape, elastic, zippers, and stencils.

• Baskets are also a fun way to store arts and craft materials. You might consider putting several craft items in a basket and giving it as a Christmas gift to a friend.

• Another gift idea is to spray glue on a "perfect box" and cover it with a patchwork of fabric pieces. It looks country and creative. In fact, you might even do it for yourself! It would be a good way to quickly see what fabrics you've stored in the box.

Now that you're all organized, you don't have to spend half your time finding supplies and setting up. You can devote your energies to what you do best—creating!

| *Child-Proof Safety in the Home*

It was early December and we were decorating our mantel for Christmas. We had just placed our handsome wooden goose, which weighs about 25 pounds, on our sturdy wood mantel. Who would have expected he could jump off and land on my right foot! The goose was repaired in a few minutes. We put a bow around his neck and placed him back in his spot. My foot? Well it took a little longer to fix—six weeks in a cast and six months before it was fully healed.

The moral of the story—don't tangle with a wooden goose! Even when we take precautions, accidents can happen. The National Safety Council estimates there is a home accident every seven seconds. Many of them can be avoided.

Shortly after our two adorable grandchildren were born, I realized again the important of making our home safe for small children. Even though we no longer have children living in our home, I don't want to take a chance of an accident when one of those precious grandchildren come for a visit. Charcoal lighter fluid might not taste good, yet a thirsty child could easily grab the can, put it to his mouth, and down a swallow in a matter of seconds. So we all need to be aware and do a little organizing now to hopefully prevent any accidents to those we love.

Let's use the following as a checklist to child-proof our homes:

Kitchen

- Keep knives in knife holders on a wall or in a high drawer.
- Place knives point down in the dishwasher.
- Cleaning powders and solutions can be stored in a plastic bucket or carryall with handle and stored on a shelf in the garage or hall closet. This can then be taken from room to room to clean, and frees up space under the kitchen and bathroom sinks for storing towels and paper products.
- Never leave a cord plugged into a socket when the other end is exposed. That's an open invitation for a baby to place the cord in his mouth.
- Use an empty toilet paper tube to store your cords, placing them in a drawer.
- When cooking on a stove top, keep handles facing the back of the stove. Children can easily dump boiling water or hot food on themselves by pulling an exposed handle or swinging a toy overhead. (Incidentally, the best way I've found to treat minor burns is to run cold water over them. Blisters don't usually appear. Raw egg whites are also good to rub on burns.)
- Always wrap broken glass in paper or place it in an old paper sack before throwing it in the trash. This is also a good rule for razor blades and the lids from metal cans. It protects a child who might inadvertently

drop a toy in the trash and try to retrieve it. Or the explorer who can't just dump the trash but has to check out every item in the process.

• When cleaning broken glass off the floor, dampen a paper towel and it will wipe up all those little pieces of glass. It protects the hands, too.

• Teach children to pour hot water slowly, aiming the stream away from themselves. Be sure to check the lid of a teapot or kettle to make sure it fits tightly and won't fall into the cup and splash boiling water.

• Any poisonous or extremely hazardous products should be kept in a locked cabinet on a very high shelf.

• Don't store products in unlabeled jars or cans. It's too easy to forget what's inside.

• Put safety covers over every exposed electrical outlet. Small children love to stick fingers and objects into these openings. These plastic caps are very inexpensive and can be purchased at drug stores, hardware stores, and many children's shops.

Bathroom

• **Never, absolutely never leave children unattended in the bathtub.** A lifeguard needs to be on duty at *all* times. There are too many hazards the youngster faces. If the doorbell or phone rings, take the child with you—or don't answer it.

• Check water temperature before putting children in the tub or shower. It might have started out warm, but gotten hotter by inadvertently brushing the knob.

• Never allow children to fiddle with the faucets. Scalds happen very quickly.

• Never add hot water to the bathtub with baby in it. Make sure the hot water faucet is turned off tightly. Wrap a washcloth around the faucet for safety when a baby or young child is in the tub.

• Teach every family member that the shower valve

is always turned OFF when finished. Otherwise a bather or bathtub cleaner risks getting scalding water on the head. (Not to mention the possibility of Mom ruining her hairdo.)

• When small children are running around the house, keep bathroom doors closed at all times. A latch placed above the knob will eliminate a major source of accidents.

• Be careful of bathroom doors that lock from the inside. Be sure you have an emergency key and know where to find it should junior lock himself in.

• Door gates are also a good way to close off a bathroom, as well as other rooms and stairs. These gates can be purchased at most stores that have baby departments. Often you can find them at garage sales or through the classified ad section of your newspaper.

Shopping with the Kids

• Make sure toddlers and smaller children are secured in the shopping cart by a cloth belt or string rope. This prevents them from standing and risking a dangerous fall. Recently I found a quilted shopping cart liner at a boutique. It fits into the seat of the cart and has a tie to hold babies and toddlers in their seats. It's cute and functional. I gave it to our daughter to use for our grandchildren. Check in your pattern books to see if they've come out with the pattern.

• Don't let your little darlings run wild in a store. Also, don't let them push the shopping cart, unless you want them to run over people and bump into shelves, counters, and food cases.

• Children often want to help you shop. But that help should not take the form of pulling items off shelves. Especially the bottom container in a beautifully-stacked pyramid of cereal boxes.

• Cans can be a danger if dropped on a foot, especially a barefooted little person. Or a child inside a cart can pick up a can and drop it outside the cart—onto Mom's toe.

• Teach children not to nag for your attention, trying to get you to buy candy or a food item they saw on television. Reward children after shopping when they've been good—with some fruit, or feeding the ducks, or time with Mom to color, draw, or play a game.

Miscellaneous

• Post emergency phone numbers in plain view by the phone for you and babysitters.

• Take a first-aid class, including CPR (cardiopulmonary resuscitation), from your local Red Cross.

• Give children swimming lessons at the earliest possible age. Many YMCA's and YWCA's offer great programs for children. If lessons aren't available, work with your children on holding their breath and blowing bubbles under water. It's fun and it will help them become comfortable in water.

• Buy or make up a first-aid kit, if you don't already have one. This is stored out of children's reach.

• Use side rails on small children's beds to keep them from falling out. These can be purchased out of catalogs or in children's departments.

• Keep scissors, plastic bags, ice picks, shish kebab skewers, fondue forks, and matches out of the reach of children.

• Warn children never to touch an electrical appliance plug with wet hands.

For more safety ideas, see *Emilie's Household Hints*, published by Harvest House Publishers.

Chapter 12

Energy-Saving Tips for Around the House

"There is precious treasure and oil in the dwelling of the wise, but a foolish man swallows it up."

Proverbs 21:20 NASB

*J*t's surprising how much our energy bills can fluctuate from month to month. Some factors are beyond our control: extreme weather, illness in the family, the location of our home, older and less efficient appliances. In addition, houseguests, home improvement projects, and vacations can contribute to the wide range of energy usage. Is there anything we can do to stabilize our bills and hold down energy costs?

Most energy users are easily recognized and we can often make them more efficient. Here are some tips to help stabilize those energy bills.

Refrigerator/Freezer

Our refrigerator/freezer is one of the largest energy users in our home. Here are a few ways to beat the cost of keeping food cool.

1. *Keep it clean.* In a manual defrost model, just a quarter of an inch of frost acts as an insulator and makes

the freezer work harder. So defrost regularly. Vacuum the condenser coils below or at the back of the appliance three or four times a year. Clean coils keep it running efficiently and help save electricity.

2. *Keep it closed.* The time for decisions is not when you have the door open. Get everything you need for a sandwich or recipe in one trip.

3. *Keep it full.* Frozen foods help keep the air cool in your freezer. However, don't overpack food in either the refrigerator or freezer because then the cold air won't circulate properly.

4. *Heat has no business in the refrigerator.* Cool dishes before you store them and your appliance won't have to work so hard.

5. *Investigate before you buy.* A frost-free refrigerator/freezer may use 30 percent more electricity than a manual defrost unit. Also, choose the right cubic footage for your size family. A too-full unit and a too-empty one both waste energy.

6. *Unplug your second refrigerator.* Refrigerators are big energy users. So if your second unit is not being used to full capacity, unplug it. That could save you $15 a month or more, depending on the size.

Range/Oven

Your food budget doesn't end at the checkout counter. These days, the cost of preparing food can add up. Here are some ways to hold down cooking costs.

1. *Pots and pans are important.* Pans with flared sides, or that are smaller than your burner, let heat escape. If a pan is too big or has a warped bottom, food won't cook evenly. For most foods, a medium-weight aluminum pan cooks faster and more efficiently. Save your heavy pans for dishes that require slow, steady cooking.

2. *Cover up.* Use pan covers. Trapped steam cooks food faster. Also, thaw frozen foods completely before cooking.

3. *Preheating is out.* Unless you're cooking breads or cakes, you do not need to preheat the oven.

4. *Plan all-oven meals.* A meal like meat loaf, baked tomatoes, scalloped potatoes, and baked apples can cook at the same time and temperature.

5. *Boiling water.* Water won't get any hotter with prolonged boiling. So if all you need is hot water for tea or drip coffee, turn off your range once the water has started to boil.

6. *Keep the oven door closed.* Every time you open the oven, you lose 25 degrees of heat. Buy a timer and be patient.

7. *Leftovers.* Your stove has leftover heat. A gas oven retains heat up to 15 minutes; an electric oven, up to half an hour; an electric range top element for three to five minutes. Use that free heat to warm up desserts or rolls, or to freshen crackers and cookies.

8. *Keep it clean.* A range free of grease and baked-on residue will work more efficiently.

9. *Use a microwave oven.* A microwave oven uses about the same amount of energy per hour as a conventional electric oven, but cooks most foods in less than half the time. That can mean a big savings on the cooking portion of your electric bill.

10. *Use your electric skillet,* broiler oven, or toaster oven instead of your electric range oven for cooking and baking in small quantities. They may use half the energy and won't heat up the kitchen.

Washer/Dryer

---

1. *Wash full loads.* Two or three large items, like sheets, with a number of small ones (but don't pack them tight) will give you a clean wash without taxing

your washer's motor. If it is necessary to wash less than a full load, adjust the water level setting accordingly.

2. *Sort by fabric, color, and degree of soil.* Use hot water only for whites, hard-to-clean items, and sterilization. Use cold or warm water on the rest. They'll be just as clean, fade less, and have fewer wrinkles.

3. *Check hose and faucet connections.* If a hose is cracked or the faucet connection is loose, you're probably losing hot water.

4. *Don't overdo.* Limit use of soap and the length of washing and drying cycles. An over-sudsed machine uses more energy. Regular clothes only need a 10- to 15-minute wash cycle. And overdrying will age clothes faster, and make them stiff and wrinkled.

5. *Clean out the lint.* Clean filters on the dryer after every use. Besides making clothes more attractive, a lint-free machine works more efficiently.

6. *Use the original solar clothes dryer.* Yes, your clothesline will definitely help your conservation efforts. It can save you between $2 and $9 off an average $70 electric bill.

Hot Water

This is the third largest energy user in the average household. But you can cut it down painlessly.

1. *Consider flow restrictor devices...* for all faucets and showers. They can cut water consumption in half.

2. *Use a water-heater insulation blanket.* That can save up to nine percent of water heater costs.

3. *Fix the drips.* One drip a second on a leaky hot-water faucet can waste up to 700 gallons of hot water a year.

4. *Shower versus bath.* If you keep your shower under five minutes, it's the winner for less hot-water use. And shampoo in the sink. A shower just to shampoo is a hot-water waster.

5. *Dishwashing.* You use ten gallons *each* time you wash dishes by hand. A dishwasher uses about 13 gallons. Try to run it once a day or less.

6. *Use cold water* for garbage disposal. It solidifies the grease and flushes it away easily.

7. *140 degrees* is an adequate setting for your hot-water heater. That's a "medium" setting if your dial isn't numbered. If you don't have a dishwasher, 120 degrees may be adequate. Set the dial on "pilot" when you go away on vacation.

Small Appliances

Some small appliances can do the same job as their full-sized counterparts at half the energy use. Use them whenever practical.

1. *Small but significant.* Small appliances use less energy if you remember to turn them off when you're through. Pull the plug on your coffee pot, iron, electric skillet, and curling iron. A memory lapse will waste energy and might ruin the appliance.

2. *Use them.* You needn't be guilt-stricken about the luxury of an electric toothbrush or carving knife. A continuous-charge toothbrush uses less than five cents a month; the carving knife, usually less than ten cents a year. Instead, cut down on using big appliances. They're the ones that add up.

Lighting

Although lights don't use much energy individually, they add up because there are so many of them and they get so much use—especially in winter. Here are some ideas for keeping lighting costs down.

1. *Fluorescent lights* provide three times the light as incandescent for the same amount of electricity. They are very economical for bathrooms and kitchens, last ten times as long, and produce less heat.

2. *Dimmer switches* can multiply bulb life up to 12 times while reducing electricity use.

3. *Lights out.* Turn them off when you're leaving a room, and teach your family to do the same. When you're away from the house, use an automatic timer to turn the lights on and off.

4. *Let the light shine through.* Lamp shades lined in white give the best light. Tall, narrow shades or short, dark shades waste watts. Dirt and dust absorb light, so add bulb-dusting to your cleaning list.

5. *One will do.* Rearrange your rooms so that one properly shaded light does the work of three or four. If you're redecorating, use light colors; dark colors absorb light.

6. *Don't use* infrared heating lights for night lights or general lighting.

7. *Use lower watt bulbs.*

8. *Turn off all outdoor lights* except those necessary for safety and security.

Air Conditioning

In many areas keeping cool in the summer can cost a lot more than keeping warm in winter. Here are some ways to keep that cost down.

1. *Degree of comfort.* Set the thermostat at 78 degrees or higher. A setting of 78 degrees saves 20 to 25 percent of your operating costs over a setting of 73 degrees.

2. *Keep it inside.* Close doors and windows. Check weatherstripping. Seal up cracks. Insulate. All of these measures will help cut cooling costs.

3. *Don't block vents.* Move furniture away from vents and window units. Trim shrubbery around outside vents.

4. *Close drapes or blinds* to keep the sun's heat out. Solar screens and shades can effectively block a large

amount of the sun's heat before it enters your home.

5. *Check the filters.* They should be checked once a month during hot weather. Vacuum or replace them as necessary.

6. *Grow deciduous trees* where they will shade your house during the heat of the day, and let the warming sun through during winter months.

7. *Check the "EER" before you buy.* Some systems use less energy than others—up to two times less. Find the Energy Efficiency Rating (EER) on the yellow energy guide label. The higher the EER, the more efficient the unit. An EER of "10" will consume half the electricity of a similar unit rated "5."

Heating

Your heating system, whether gas or electric, is probably your home's biggest energy user in winter. It can be an energy waster if you're not wise.

1. *Leave the thermostat alone* during the day. Set it at 65 degrees or below. Operating costs rise five percent every time you raise the thermostat two degrees. Turn it down to 55 degrees or off altogether at bedtime. Let a timer turn it back on before you rise.

2. *Check the filter* once a month and replace or clean as necessary.

3. *Proper insulation* keeps your home warm in winter, cool in summer. In fact, up to 20 percent of your heating energy can be lost through an uninsulated ceiling.

4. *Cut more heat loss* by weatherstripping doors and windows. Close the damper when not using the fireplace or heat will escape. Close off rooms not in use along with their heating vents. But don't close off more than 30 percent of the house. Make sure you leave the vent open near the thermostat to insure proper temperature control. Turn off individual thermostats. And

remind everyone to cooperate by keeping outside doors closed.

5. *Close draperies at night* to keep out the cold. Open them during the day to let the sunshine in.

6. *Turn off electric heat* at the circuit breaker if you want to make sure it is off.

Swimming Pool

If you have a pool, a major portion of your energy outlay is the cost of operating it. Here are some ways to control those energy costs.

1. *Lower the pool's temperature.* Lowering the pool heater setting from 80 degrees to 78 degrees could save up to 20 percent in heating costs. The lower temperature saves on chemicals, too.

2. *Use a swimming pool cover.* You can save as much as 80 percent of your summer pool heating bill with a pool cover.

3. *Heat early in the morning.* Sun and pool heaters work together more efficiently during morning hours.

4. *Protect your pool from wind.* Wind has the same effect on your pool as blowing on hot soup. Hedges, fences, and cabanas help keep wind down.

5. *Don't overfilter.* Most pools require only four to five hours of filtering a day in summer, and two to three hours in winter. Reducing your filtration by 50 percent may save more than $20 per month. Be sure to filter before 11 A.M. and/or after 5 P.M.

6. *Keep filter, skimmer, and strainer basket clean.* When your pump motor doesn't work as hard, it costs less to operate.

7. *Don't overclean.* Automatic pool sweeping devices can usually do the job in three to four hours a day in summer, two to three hours per day in the off season. But remember to set the cleaner to start 15 minutes

before your filter, and try to operate the sweep outside the hours of 11 A.M. to 5 P.M.

Water Bed

Water bed energy costs could make you lose sleep if not controlled.

1. *Don't unplug the bed during the day.* Getting the bed up to temperature every night uses more energy than operating it continuously with thermostat control.

2. *Make the bed every morning.* Controlled tests have shown that beds with mattress pad sheets, cotton quilt, one blanket, and a one-inch foam rubber mat between mattress and pad save about $15 a month over one covered only by sheets.

Chapter 13

Cleaning and Organizing the Garage

> *"There is an appointed time for everything."*
>
> Ecclesiastes 3:1 NASB

"**H**elp! Come fast! Here, in the garage! I'm buried under the newspapers and magazines."

Ever felt like that? Maybe you've actually had a pile of clutter collapse around you in the garage . . . or lived in fear of such an occurrence. That's when you know you can no longer postpone the big event. You really must clean the garage.

Where do we begin in this awesome task? Well, the first thing you need to do is set a date and time. Call a family meeting and ask the family to help "poor Mom" clean the garage. Agree on the date—say next Saturday at 9:00 A.M.—and mark it clearly on your calendar. No absences are excused!

Then as the big day draws closer, assemble the following items:

- Trash bags.
- Jars—mayonnaise, peanut butter, and jelly size.
- Small metal cabinets with plastic drawers. You

can purchase these at a hardware store. These can take the place of the jars.

- Large hooks—the type on which you can hang bicycles.
- Boxes—cardboard-type used for apples and oranges. Most supermarkets have them. (Many stores tear the boxes apart as soon as they are emptied. You may want to ask ahead to see if the produce manager can save a few for you.) "Perfect boxes" are great for storage and display of materials.
- Broom and rake hooks. These can also be purchased at hardware stores.
- One to four plastic trash cans—for uses *other* than trash.
- Two to six empty coffee cans.
- Black marking pen.
- Three plastic trash bags marked "Put Away," "Throw Away," and "Give Away."

That's right! We're moving from Total Mess to Total Rest. The principles are similar for every area of our home. We're attacking the garage separately because it often escapes the scrutiny of the rest of our house. Surely organizing this space can relieve some more of our stress.

There's a little more preparation you need to do for the big day. First, make a list of all the jobs required. Then delegate responsibilities to each member of the family. Or, these responsibilities can be written on pieces of paper and placed in a basket. On the big day, have each family member (plus friends and neighbors— recruit as much help as you want and make it a party!) draw one or more jobs from the basket. Keep going around until all the jobs are assigned. Here's an example:

Jenny: Sort all nails, screws, nuts, and washers into

different jars or in the metal organization cabinet you purchased.

Brad: Separate tools—hammers, screwdrivers, wrenches, etc. Put them into the empty coffee cans you have prelabeled with the black marking pen.

Dad: Sort your possessions—papers, pipes, power tools, etc.—and place them in jars and cardboard boxes. Label containers with the black marking pen.

Craig: Neatly roll up the hoses, extension cords, wires, ropes, and any other roll-up type of material. Put all gardening tools with long handles—rake, shovel, edger, broom—into one of the trash cans, or hang these tools on a wall in the garage, using the specially-purchased hooks.

Micky: Empty the large bag of dried dog food into another of the plastic trash cans and cover with a tight lid. This will keep the food fresh and prevent mice and other little animals from enjoying it.

Mark: Collect all the rags, old towels, and sheets and fold neatly into a trash can or a cardboard box. Mark the container accordingly. Make sure none of the rags are saturated with a flammable substance (they should be tossed). This job should be done away from the flame of a water heater or furnace.

Mom: Arrange and label the cardboard boxes and store them on shelves. You might want to organize according to priority. For example, you don't need the Christmas ornaments on a lower shelf since they're used only once a year. (See Chapter 5 for more details.)

Everyone can help fill the "Put Away," "Throw Away," and "Give Away" trash bags. You might want to designate yourself as the final arbitrator in case of indecision. But make sure the bags are used. You'll find old newspapers, magazines, empty or dried-up cans of paint. These things should be thrown away.

Bicycles can be hung on the rafters with the large

hooks you purchased at the hardware store. Most cars can park easily under them in the average garage. If some of the bicycles are used every day, then maybe Dad or an older son can make a bike rack.

Partially-used bags of cement, fertilizer, and other dry materials can be stored in the plastic trash cans with lids. This will keep the materials dry.

Items such as gardening pots, bricks, and flats can be neatly stored on a shelf or outside the garage. You might build a few outside shelves for that purpose. Winter weather won't harm them, and you have little need for them during those months anyway.

Now, don't you feel better just knowing that the garage can be cleaned and organized? Then get your calendar out, call the family together, and decide when!

Chapter 14 | Let's Have a Garage Sale

"Any enterprise is built by wise planning, becomes strong through common sense, and profits wonderfully by keeping abreast of the facts."

Proverbs 24:3,4 TLB

The summer is almost over, the kids are restless, and you've had it with all the clutter. Why not plan a garage sale? Tell the kids they can keep the money from the sale of their items. You'll be amazed how quickly they are motivated to clean their rooms and get rid of clutter.

If you have school-age children at home, an annual garage sale is a must. It's the best way to motivate the family to clean out the garage, closets, and bedrooms. Most families are storing things they never use, taking up space in closets, shelves, cupboards, and under the bed.

When our kids lived at home, we'd talk about purchasing school supplies and new clothes a few weeks before school started. We'd make lists and estimate what it would cost to equip and outfit each child. That led naturally into planning our garage sale as a way to help finance back-to-school needs. We'd all get excited about the possibility of selling outgrown clothes, unused items, books, and old toys.

Back-to-school wasn't the only way to spend the money we'd raise. We would discuss as a family other ways to use the money. Sometimes we agreed to give a portion to a missionary family, a church project, or the building fund. And the children would use some of the money they earned from selling their items to buy a new game or book they especially wanted. This was a great teaching tool to help them learn how to earn, give, spend, and save money.

Set the Date

It's best to make your garage sale for one day only, either on a Friday or Saturday.

Once the date is set, call the newspaper or community shopper and place an ad. The ad should be short. Do *not* include your phone number. It only produces a lot of unnecessary calls with silly questions. Here's a sample ad:

> GARAGE SALE—Saturday, September 6, 9:00 A.M. to 5:00 P.M. Bookcase, toys, antiques, appliances, clothing, bike, tools, and lots of goodies. 2838 Rumsey Drive, Central Avenue at Victoria.

Now that you've placed the ad, you're committed. You've got to follow through and make it happen.

Making and Placing the Signs

Use heavy cardboard or brightly colored posterboard and bold felt-tip pens in contrasting colors. For example, if your board is yellow, use a black or dark blue pen.

Keep the signs simple. You don't need to list items. You only need the words GARAGE SALE in large letters, plus your street address. Many cars are like mine—

they go on automatic when we see one of those signs—
and before you know it, the car is parked right in front
of that house.

Place your signs in prominent locations. Use your
own stakes. Do not attach them to street or speed-limit
signs. And when your sale is finished, always go back
and remove the signs.

Deciding What to Sell

Now you need to clean house and decide what to
sell. Spend time with each child and go over the items
they begin to pull out of their rooms. Sometimes in the
enthusiasm of the event, they decide to sell their bed,
favorite teddy bear, even the cat or dog. You can help
evaluate what goes, but be careful not to get too car-
ried away yourself.

Once I got so excited that I sold our refrigerator.
People were coming by and buying so many things that
I stopped thinking clearly. I didn't like our refrigerator, anyway, and we were selling so many items and
bringing in a lot of money. . .well, when someone
asked what else I had for sale, I said, "How about the
refrigerator?" It sold immediately. I was thrilled until
Bob got home and heard the news. Let's just say I
learned a good lesson.

Organization

Display sale items in categories. All the toys should
go in one place, glassware and kitchen utensils in
another, and so forth. Use tables—picnic tables and card
tables are good—to display breakable items. You might
want to cover the table tops with butcher paper or old
tablecloths to give a tidy appearance.

Have an extension cord available from a garage or
house outlet so people can check any electrical appliances such as popcorn popper, iron, razor, or clock.

If the item doesn't work, tell the truth. Your interested customer may still buy it. Many garage-sale shoppers are handymen who can fix anything or salvage use-able parts. Never underestimate what will sell. Don't say, "That's junk" and trash it. There are many creative people who will buy your "junk."

Cover not-for-sale items with old sheets or tarps. People will buy everything in the garage if you're not careful. You may need to make a few NOT FOR SALE signs, especially if the children's bikes are in open view.

Hospitality adds to the garage sale. Try serving hot coffee, tea, or ice tea. This is particularly nice during the first couple of hours in the morning.

Set Your Price

Pricing takes some time and thought. As a general rule, keep the prices down. Never mark directly on the article. If husband's shirt doesn't sell, he may go to the office one day with "$1.50" inked on the cuff or pocket. Stick-on labels, round stickers, or masking tape work best.

If individual family members are going to keep the money from the sale of certain items, be sure to mark those items with appropriate initials or color code. (Linda's the blue label, Tom's green, Krista's yellow, Erik's red.)

I like to price everything in fifty-cent increments. That gives you some bargaining power. Even with your low prices, people love to try and bring the price a lit-tle lower.

You might have separate boxes with items priced 5 cents, 10 cents, and 25 cents. This will save you from having to mark each individual item. You might even have a box marked FREE. Children love these boxes because they can shop while Mom and Dad look around.

Have one person, preferably an adult, be the cashier. All purchases go through that person. On a large sheet of poster board, list each person who is selling at your sale. As each item is sold, remove the price sticker and place it under his or her name, or write the price in the appropriate column. At the end of the day, just add each column and you're ready to divide the spoils.

By the way, it's best to accept only cash from your customers. Checks are okay if you know the person, but don't feel obligated. You don't have the advantage of a store that can match check numbers against a list of those whose checks have bounced.

Make Time Count

On the day of the sale, get up early and commit the day to the sale. We've found that people who know antiques and other valuable items hit the garage sales early, often the day before or an hour before you open. So be prepared and have everything set up the day before. When it's time, simply move the tables and other items outside onto the walkway, patio, or driveway.

Eat a good breakfast. You'll need a clear mind for bargain decisions. And pack lunches for you and your children the night before. You won't have time to make lunch when people are in your yard all day.

When you're done, keep in the festive mood and plan something special like a barbecue or have dinner out with some of the proceeds. It will put an appropriate finish on a wonderful day.

What do you do with the items that don't sell? The one thing you *don't* want to do is bring them back into your home. Remember, these are items you no longer use, need, or want. So place all the unsold items in bags or boxes and call an organization such as Salvation Army or Goodwill. They'll usually come and pick up the items. Be sure to get a receipt for a tax deduction.

Finally, don't forget to remove the signs you put up around the neighborhood to draw all those customers. It's best to do this as soon as the sale is over, or at latest, first thing the next morning.

Block Garage Sales

Many neighborhoods plan an annual garage sale involving several families on one street. This is an exciting tradition that draws a lot of interest in the participants as well as bargain hunters.

The organizational principles are the same. It involves at least one joint planning meeting so all the details can be discussed. Review all the particulars so the day runs smoothly.

You might want to appoint a committee to design and place the ad in the local newspaper announcing the sale. Be sure to emphasize that it is a *neighborhood* garage sale. That will draw a lot more interest from the shoppers. A joint sign-making committee will also save time and duplication of work.

It is very important that all families are ready when the sale starts.

An enjoyable end-of-day activity is to have a joint barbecue for all the participants. This builds neighborhood spirit and breaks down barriers you might have. Some neighborhoods have even had the local police department barricade off the block so the party can be held in the street. It's a lot of fun and a different way to have a party.

Ready to have a sale? Exhibit U is a checklist to help you prepare.

'Garage Sale' Checklist

ASSIGNMENT	DONE	COMMENT
1. Need for garage sale has been established.	✓	May 31st
2. Date has been set.	✓	May 31st
3. Ad has been placed in local newspaper.		Monday before sale.
4. Signs are made.	✓	
5. Signs are posted.		Evening before sale.
6. Signs are removed after garage sale.		
7. Garage is cleaned out. A. Child #1—Bedroom cleaned out B. Child #2—Bedroom cleaned out C. Child #3—Bedroom cleaned out D. _____ E. _____		The Saturday before sale.
8. Items for sale are assembled in one section of the garage or patio.		To be completed Wednesday before.
9. Display tables are identified.	✓	

EXHIBIT U

ASSIGNMENT	DONE	COMMENT

10. Day before sale:
  A. Price all items
  B. Set up tables
  C. Display items in categories
  D. Plug in extension cord (testing of appliances)
  E. Cover non-sale items with sheets or tarps
		To do on Friday.

F. Make your large display board to keep track of individual sales account
  G. Make lunch for tomorrow
  H. Other _____
  _____
  _____		

11. Day of sale:
  A. Wake up early
  B. Post signs
  C. Move tables out of garage to sidewalks
  D. Coffee/tea is a nice gesture for the shoppers
  E. Have an adult or older child handle the "money box"
  F. As item is sold, credit the "account chart" under proper seller's name (see Account Chart)
		To be done Saturday.

ASSIGNMENT	DONE	COMMENT
G. Have a "quiet and gentle spirit"		
H. Place all the remaining items in bags or boxes. Call Salvation Army or Goodwill to come and pick up. Obtain receipt for tax deduction.		
I. Clean up		
J. Remove signs from neighborhood		
K. Clean up with a bath or shower		
L. Plan to have a barbecue (or maybe even dinner out)		*Hamburger Fry.*
M. Divide the profits for the day		
N. Evaluate the day		

Account Chart

DAD	MOM	BRAD	CRAIG	JENNY	CHRIS	CHAD
1.50	.50	.25	.50	2.00	.50	1.00
.75	1.00	1.00	2.50	1.50	1.00	.50
1.00	.50	1.50	1.00	.50	1.00	.50
						1.50
Totals:						
3.25	2.00	2.75	4.00	4.00	2.50	3.50

Chapter 15

Enjoying the Holidays

> *"He who observes the day, observes it for the Lord, and he who eats, does so for the Lord, for he gives thanks to God."*
>
> Romans 14:6 NASB

*E*very year, for many years, I asked myself the same questions: "Why is preparing for Thanksgiving and Christmas always so hectic?" and "Why can't I plan ahead and just once get a holiday meal on the table on time?" In talking with many other women, I find that the holidays, which should be the most enjoyable days of the year, are often the most stressful. I can't say I've got this area completely under control. But I've learned a few tricks in three areas—meal preparation, gifts, and wrapping—that can ease much of our stress.

Let's tackle the hardest one first—holiday meals.

Step 1: Make the Guest List

If your Thanksgiving or Christmas dinner includes family members who live away from home, invite them early in the month and specify the time of day you would like them to arrive.

A wonderful way to share Thanksgiving is to extend

an invitation to a neighborhood family or several young couples. Especially remember young single adults, orphans, foreign students, widow/widowers, or single-parent families when planning your holiday celebrations. Thanksgiving and Christmas are often particularly lonely times for these people, especially when they are separated from loved ones.

Step 2: Plan the Menu

Early in the month, decide every item you will serve, from hors d'oeuvres to dessert. If family and friends offer to help, assign them each a specific dish. Give them the recipes if you have particular ones planned. Large families often make their holiday meals potluck to relieve the pressure on one individual. Try to keep the meal festive yet simple. Now is not the time to attempt a new recipe.

Step 3: Compile the Grocery List

As you plan your menu, list all the ingredients you will need. This will give you three weeks to purchase the necessary supplies, allowing you to look for sales on many of the items.

Be sure to remember garnishes, such as watercress and parsley. To keep both parsley and watercress fresh, wash them and put them stems down in a jar. Pour about an inch of water into the jar, enough for the stems to stand without the leaves getting wet. Put a tight lid on the jar and store in the refrigerator. These garnishes will stay crisp for up to two weeks.

Step 4: Prepare Ahead

As much as possible, bake or prepare all menu items ahead of the big day. Schedule a baking day to prepare your homemade rolls, bread, and pie crusts and freeze them. If you plan a vegetable platter for hors d'oeuvres, clean and cut the vegetables, mix the dip, and refrigerate both a couple of days ahead. Involve the family as much as possible. Children especially love to help in the kitchen and this time can provide a positive learning experience for them.

Step 5: Seven-Day Checklist

Day 7:
- Order turkey, ham, goose, or whatever meat you plan to serve.
- If you are renting tables, chairs, or other equipment, arrange for rental and pickup.

Day 6:
- Choose table linens and be sure they are washed and ironed.
- Check supply of serving dishes and borrow any needed items.
- Read over recipes to be sure grocery list is complete.
- Estimate cooking times and list them next to each recipe.

Day 5:
- Determine seating plan and make name cards. (To keep with the thankful spirit, you might write a Scripture verse of thanksgiving under each name.)

Day 4:
- Sharpen carving knives.
- Shop for fresh produce you plan to prepare ahead of time.
- Prepare recipes that can be refrigerated or frozen.

Day 3:
- Complete any unfinished grocery shopping.
- Clean house.
- Bake pies.

Day 2:
- Pick up turkey, ham, or other meat.
- Prepare centerpiece arrangements from a variety of fruits, vegetables, candles, pumpkins, natural leaves, and nuts. Or purchase fresh flowers.
- Set the table.
- For an added festive touch, set a fresh plant or flower in the guest bathroom.

Day 1:
- Delegate responsibilities. Make sure each family member knows exactly what to do.
- Stuff your bird and place in the oven. Be sure to allow enough time for it to cool before carving.
- Do a quick check of the house to make sure everything is in order.
- Finish last-minute cooking.
- Put on a clean apron.
- Smile and thank God for this special day when you can enjoy your family and friends.

We have always found that as we gather around the table, it is important to take a few moments to thank God for His many abundant gifts to us. Sometimes we have each person read the Scripture verse on his or her name card. Or we have everyone share one thing he or she is thankful for. This is a time to enjoy each other, a good meal, and most important, our relationship with God.

Easy Gift Ideas for Christmas

Some people have no trouble thinking of appropriate gifts for their friends and family. Others find it hard to be creative. And most of us want to make sure the spending doesn't get out of hand.

When I was a little girl, my mother taught me how to make fun, yet inexpensive gifts. Over the years, I've accumulated a list of creative gift ideas, so I'm never left wondering what to do for that person "who has everything" or when thinking, "I have no idea what she needs." Here are a few of those ideas for your next Christmas.

• Give a favorite recipe, written on a cute card, and include two or three of the ingredients. An example: a recipe for chocolate-chip oatmeal cookies, one package of chocolate chips, one package of nuts, and two cups of oatmeal in a zip-lock bag.

• Take baby food jars and apply cute stickers to the jars and lids. Three of these make a nice gift for storing such things as cotton balls, bath salts, and cotton swabs.

• Paint "Honey Pot" on the front of a jar, fill with honey, and tie a cute ribbon around the lid.

• Make Christmas ornaments out of different kinds of noodles, using white glue.

• Cover a shoe box with wrapping paper, wallpaper, or contact paper, and use as a gift box filled with stationery items like a glue stick, small scissors, paper clips, marking pens, memo pad, and thank-you notes. Any mom, dad, grandparent, or teacher would appreciate such a gift.

• Cover a box with road maps and fill the box with maps, a first-aid kit, a teaching or music tape, jumper cables, flares, or any item associated with travel or the car.

• Baskets make great gifts when filled with items like:

Bath—soaps, shower cap, bubble bath, bath oil, washcloth.

Reading—a book for each family member, bookmarks.

Kitchen—wooden spoons, measuring cups, can opener. . .

Toys—games, books, teddy bear, doll, truck, puzzle. . .

Grandma—bib and other baby items for grand-babies, book of short stories. . .

Gardening—seeds, garden tools, gloves, pruning clippers, potted plants, hand shovel.

Sewing—measuring tape, scissors, pins, jar of buttons, elastic, lace, ribbon, tape. . .

Laundry—bleach, laundry powder or liquid, fabric softener, spray 'n' wash, small spot brush.

For Men—car wax, chamois, trash bags, litter bag for car, coffee mug for car, travel kit. . .

• Food items always make great gifts, especially when you use resources available in your area. For example, those who live in Florida or Arizona might give baskets of citrus fruit. We have several orange trees on our property and every year I fill a box or basket of oranges and send them to my uncle. He loves the gift and always looks forward to it. Every year a friend gives us a bag of raw peanuts which we enjoy for several months. Here are other food-gift ideas:

> Popcorn
> Banana or zucchini bread
> Nuts—almonds, walnuts, hazel nuts
> Carmel corn
> Pure maple syrup
> Fruits—apples, dates, pears...
> Avocados
> Dried fruits
> Natural foods such as granola mix or 3-7 grain cereal
> Bread starters
> Homemade jams, jellies, relish...
> Spiced tea mixes

Many of these gifts can be prepared way ahead of time, relieving you of added pressure as the Christmas season approaches.

Another part of the fun of Christmas is in the wrapping, especially when we use a little ingenuity.

Organize the Wrapping Center

Concealing your niece's teddy bear in the Sunday funnies or placing a jar of homemade apricot preserves in a decorated gift sack for Aunt Elma makes the recipients of your gifts feel you've given their wrappings individual attention. However, such originality requires some organization. Designate an area of your home for gift wrapping. Set up a table such as a card table a couple of weeks before Christmas. On the table place a box filled with materials like:

Scissors
Scotch tape (double-stick is especially handy)
Mailing tape
String or twine
Stickers and rubber stamps
Clear cellophane and tissue paper
Wrapping paper and ribbons

To reduce waste, purchase wrapping paper on tubes. Solid colors give more flexibility, allowing you to use plaid, striped, or contrasting ribbons.

Wrapping Ideas

1. Use newspaper:
   - Funnies—use brightly colored ribbons and tie on a few bells for children's gifts.
   - Sports page—use a plaid ribbon and draw a football helmet with a red or green felt marking pen.
   - Travel section—Use ribbons to outline the shape of a favorite place to vacation.
2. Use solid, colored, shiny enamel paper:
   - For a special look, decorate your package by tying on a small pine cone or holly sprig with green or red ribbon. Or use plaid ribbon and tie on a cookie cutter shaped like a star, Christmas tree, or teddy bear.
   - Plain white paper allows you to create your own design using a rubber stamp or homemade stamp carved from a raw potato or bar of soap. Or attach a silk poinsettia or Christmas ornament to the package with a ribbon of any color.

3. Use colored cellophane:

Cellophane is especially handy for those "How in the world am I ever going to wrap this?" dilemmas.

- Line a basket, fill it with goodies and tie it with a fluffy bow and/or a sprig of holly or pine.
- Wrap cookies (or breads, jams, muffins) on a Christmas plate and tie with a cheerful bow.
- Wrap it around a plant or fresh bouquet of flowers and add a beautiful bow and card.

4. Gift sacks (A great idea when you need to quick-wrap):

- Line your sack with a contrasting tissue, or wrap your gift item in tissue and place it in the bag.
- Tie a bow around the top, attaching your gift tag.
- Add shredded tissue to the top of your sack for a party look.
- Decorate the sack with festive stickers or cut-outs from old Christmas cards.

5. Gift boxes:

Decorated gift boxes are another quick way to wrap a present. All you need to add is a bow and you're set. Always pick up a courtesy box, tissue, and ribbon whenever you purchase something at a department store where gift wrapping is free. Store these in your wrapping center. Usually they fold flat and are easy to save.

6. Other ideas:

- Shelf paper, fabric remnants, and wallpaper make good wrapping materials.
- Cut up last year's Christmas cards for unique tags and enclosure cards.
- Satin and plaid fabric make great ribbons. Cut in strips and iron between wax paper to stiffen.

- Last year's ribbons can be freshened by running them through a curling iron.
- The following items make good packing material:

> Styrofoam
> Excelsine (straw-type material)
> Easter grass (clear or colored)
> Tissue
> Dry-cleaning garment bags
> Crumpled newspaper
> Popcorn

Mailing Packages

- Each package should have at least two inches of tight packing around it, top and bottom, to ensure its safety.
- Stuff styrofoam "popcorn" pieces in your bows, or place a strawberry basket or piece of cardboard over the bow to save it from getting crushed.
- Tape your gift box securely and then wrap it tightly with mailing paper or a sturdy grocery sack. Postal officials suggest placing an address label on the gift package itself before wrapping in mailing paper. This will insure proper delivery should the covering be torn and the outside address label lost.
- Put strapping tape over all seams and folded ends.
- Stick on a mailing label with name and address and cover with a piece of clear tape to avoid moisture smearing the address.
- Decorate your package with rubber stamps, stickers, or colored felt pens, but be careful not to detract from the address.

It takes a little more time to wrap your gifts uniquely. However, the extra effort will say, ''You are special; I care about you.'' And isn't that what we want to communicate during the Christmas season?

Chapter 16 | *Baby-Sitting Survival Guide*

> *"I will instruct you and teach you in the way which you should go; I will counsel you with My eye upon you."*
>
> Psalm 32:8 NASB

Sixteen-year-old Lynn arrived at the Merrihew home eager to take care of Craig and Jenny's two adorable toddlers. The three of them talked briefly, then Craig and Jenny practically skipped out the door, delighted to have their first "date" in six weeks.

Forty-five minutes later, two-year-old Christine was still crying and screaming "Mommy!" Lynn remembered that Craig and Jenny were going to three different places that evening, but couldn't remember when they would be there. She wasn't even sure if she should call. Meanwhile, Craig and Jenny kept remembering things they wished they'd told Lynn. Their intimate conversation was interrupted by an ongoing debate about whether or not they should call home.

Whether our baby-sitter is 16 or 66, there are certain things we can do to insure a smoother and more enjoyable evening for both sitter and parents.

For Mom and Dad

• Leave a pad and pen by the phone so the sitter can note phone messages and information about the evening's events.

• Have a first-time sitter arrive a few minutes early so you and your children can get acquainted with him or her. Also, give her a brief tour of the pertinent parts of the house—children's rooms, bathroom, location of TV, location of first-aid and other supplies.

• Explain home rules about snacking, visitors, use of television or stereo, etc.

• Tell sitter what time each child goes to bed, and whether a child has a special routine—a favorite story to be read, a special blanket, a prayer time. Better yet, put these instructions in writing and keep them handy for each sitter.

• If necessary, show sitter procedures for feeding, warming bottle, and changing diapers.

• If a child is taking medication, leave a measuring spoon or dropper and written instructions concerning time and dosage next to the bottle.

* Let a sitter know at the time of initial contact whether he or she will be expected to prepare and serve a meal.

• Have a flashlight or candle handy in case of power failure.

• If the sitter cannot easily reach you, plan to call home periodically.

• If you are unable to arrive home when you said you would, call and let the sitter know you will be late and when to expect you.

• Always be prepared to pay the sitter the previously-agreed-upon fee when you return home, unless you have worked out some other arrangement ahead of time. Remember that checks are sometimes hard for teenagers to cash. Some parents pay extra for hours after midnight.

- If you must cancel a sitter at the last minute, it is courteous to pay the sitter for part of the time they were expected to sit.

- If you want the sitter to do any housework, make special arrangements at the time you hire her. Most parents pay extra for such service.

You might want to make up a printed information sheet for your sitters. Exhibit V is one idea for such a sheet. It has room for emergency phone numbers and special instructions as well as a place for the sitter to leave any comments about the evening.

As far as what is expected from a sitter, you might want to photocopy these and give them to a new sitter before you hire her.

For the Baby-Sitter

- Be sure you understand what is expected of you. Don't count on your memory; write down instructions if the list gets too long.

- Be sure you know where the parents or other adults such as grandparents or an aunt or uncle can be reached at all times.

- It is best if the children are present when parents give you instructions so everyone understands the rules.

- Don't open the door for strangers.

- Keep outside doors locked at all times.

- Deliveries can be left outside, or delivered later when parents are home.

- Never tell phone-callers that parents are not at home. Take a message, if possible.

- Keep your own phone calls brief.

- Always clean up your own messes. The extra effort you make will encourage the parents to call you again.

- Don't snoop in closets or drawers. Even though

BABY-SITTER'S INFORMATION SHEET

We can be reached at: _____

We will be home about _____ **o' clock.**

A little about us:

    Our name: _____

    Our address: _____

    Our phone number: _____

    Children's names: _____

    Ages: _____

Emergency numbers:

    Doctor: _____

    Dentist: _____

    Police: _____

    Fire/Rescue: _____

    Poison Control: _____

    Neighbor: _____

Special Instructions:

- Location of thermostat _____
- Instructions about pets _____
- Location of children's food and clothing _____
  _____
- Children's habits _____
  _____
- Bedtime/Naptime _____
  _____

Children behaved:

_____ Above Average

_____ Average

_____ Needs Improvement

Comments: _____

_____

_____

_____

EXHIBIT V

you are working in the home, you are still a guest.

• Try to stay alert and awake unless it is a long, late evening.

• Let parents know of any illness or accident, however minor. Accidents will happen and most parents allow for this.

• If you have to cancel, let parents know as soon as possible.

• It's a good idea to take a first-aid course at your local YWCA, Red Cross, or community service department. Some cities have regular classes designed for baby-sitters. If yours doesn't, buy a first-aid handbook.

Chapter 17

Organizing a Memorable Vacation

"Teach us to number our days and recognize how few they are; help us to spend them as we should."

Psalm 90:12 TLB

As a child who grew up with a single parent, I never experienced summer vacations. I have no memories of travel or special family activities in new, exotic places. So with my husband and children it was hard, at first, for me to learn how to relax and enjoy our vacation trips. In fact, we spent several summer vacations at Forest Home Christian Conference Center in southern California. There are many similar camps throughout the United States that provide great spiritual teaching, food, entertainment, and fun for every member of the family. It's a balanced vacation with a purpose, all preplanned for you.

I needed that kind of structure for a while. But I also began to realize that we could organize our own family fun. We could fly a kite over the Grand Canyon or ride bikes over the Golden Gate Bridge in San Francisco or roller skate in New York City. We could meet new friends while camping, waterskiing, and beachcombing.

However, vacations don't just happen. When traveling with children on land, sea, or air, it is vital to think ahead to prevent "disaster" experiences. If we don't, even short trips can leave the whole family exhausted and in need of a *real* vacation.

Plan as a Family

Vacations are best planned by the entire family, including the children. Some evening after dinner, have a brainstorming session. Allow everyone to be creative and suggest people, places, and things they want to see and experience. Don't limit your ideas. Think of activities that will allow every family member to experience and learn something new. Perhaps some of your ideas may not be practical for this year or in the immediate future. But it is fun to dream, and you never know. . . with all these great ideas in mind, maybe that once-in-a-lifetime dream vacation can be fulfilled.

On another evening, take some time to communicate your family vacation needs for the coming summer. Allow each family member to express his or her desire. Does one person want total rest? Another beautiful scenery? Water sports? Hiking or mountain climbing? All of the above? A balance of rest and activity?

Now we've got a list of needs and a list of potential vacations. The fun is in trying to see how we can match each person's needs with one or more vacation ideas. The more the children can participate, the better. Let them help on researching, looking at maps, planning the itinerary. If the children help plan the vacation, there will be less complaints like, "How long till we get there?" or "Do we have to do this?"

Plan Ahead

Once you've decided on the area(s) you want to visit, gather as much information as you can about that area.

Remember to find out the negatives as well as the positives so you can avoid potential problems.

• Write or call the Chamber of Commerce or a visitor/tourist bureau in the area you plan to visit for literature giving specific recommendations for family vacations.

• Contact your auto club or travel agent for maps and information about the area you plan to cover.

• Talk with friends or people who have been where you plan to visit.

• Use the checklists in Exhibits W and X to help you remember all the details.

Reservations and Arrangements

Make advance reservations at campgrounds, motels, and special tourist attractions as needed. Auto club and travel agents can alert you of where you need reservations.

• Make sure you have written confirmation of your reservations, and carry them with you as you travel.

• If you're going to be late at a lodging or campsite, you can often guarantee your reservation by prepayment of the first night's stay.

• If you must cancel a reservation, do so as early as possible so you can get total refunds and allow others to take your place. A 48-hour notice will usually insure you total refunds.

• When making reservations, check on lodging policies to see if children can sleep in parents' room at no extra charge.

• If you need a crib, reserve one at the time you make the reservation.

• When driving, begin your trip early in the morning so that you can arrive in time for everyone to relax, take a swim, or enjoy a short walk. Allow

TRAVEL & VACATION
CHECK LIST

Destination: _____

Airlines: _____ **Flight #:** _____
Depart/Date & Time: _____
Arrival/Date & Time: _____
Airlines: _____ **Flight #:** _____
Depart/Date & Time: _____
Arrival/Date & Time: _____
Airlines: _____ **Flight #:** _____
Depart/Date & Time: _____
Arrival/Date & Time: _____

Accommodations: _____
  Address: _____
  Phone: _____
  Children: _____

  Pets: _____
Deliveries To Be Stopped: _____

Mail: _____

Special Purchases For Trip: _____

Recommended Activities: _____

Recommended Restaurants: _____

Notes: _____
_____
_____
_____

EXHIBIT W

TRAVEL & VACATION
PACKING LIST

Clothing
- [ ] Belts
- [ ] Blouses
- [ ] Boots
- [ ] Bras
- [ ] Coats
- [ ] Dresses
- [ ] Gloves
- [ ] Gowns
- [ ] Handkerchiefs
- [ ] Hats
- [ ] Jackets
- [ ] Jeans
- [ ] Jewelry
- [ ] Nightgowns
- [ ] Pajamas
- [ ] Pantyhose
- [ ] Raincoat
- [ ] Robes
- [ ] Scarves
- [ ] Shirts
- [ ] Shoes
- [ ] Skirts
- [ ] Slacks
- [ ] Slippers
- [ ] Slips
- [ ] Socks
- [ ] Suits
- [ ] Sweaters
- [ ] Swimsuits
- [ ] Ties
- [ ] Underwear

Toiletries & Grooming Aids
- [ ] Aftershave
- [ ] Body Creams & Lotions
- [ ] Comb
- [ ] Cotton Balls
- [ ] Dental Floss
- [ ] Deodorant
- [ ] Electric Shaver

- [ ] Face Creams & Lotions
- [ ] Hair Brush
- [ ] Hair Clips/Pins
- [ ] Hair Conditioner
- [ ] Hair Dryer
- [ ] Hair Rollers
- [ ] Hair Spray
- [ ] Magnifying Mirror
- [ ] Makeup
- [ ] Manicure Items
- [ ] Mouthwash
- [ ] Nail Brush
- [ ] Perfume/Cologne
- [ ] Razor Blades
- [ ] Shampoo/Rinse
- [ ] Shower Cap
- [ ] Soap/Soap Dish
- [ ] Sunburn Preventive
- [ ] Talc
- [ ] Toothbrush
- [ ] Toothpaste
- [ ] Tweezers

Medications & Health Aids
- [ ] Prescription Medication
- [ ] Bandages
- [ ] Antihistamine
- [ ] Birth Control
- [ ] Calamine Lotion
- [ ] Cotton-tipped Swabs
- [ ] Diarrhea Medicine
- [ ] Electric Heating Pad
- [ ] Eye Drops
- [ ] Foot Powder
- [ ] Indigestion Remedy
- [ ] Insect Repellent

- [ ] Laxative
- [ ] Motion Sickness Remedy
- [ ] Nasal Spray
- [ ] Pain Reliever
- [ ] Rubbing Alcohol
- [ ] Sanitary Napkins
- [ ] Sleeping Pills
- [ ] Thermometer
- [ ] Tranquilizers
- [ ] Vitamins

Miscellaneous
- [ ] Address Book
- [ ] Alarm Clock
- [ ] Batteries
- [ ] Briefcase
- [ ] Calculator
- [ ] Camera/Film
- [ ] Cash
- [ ] Checkbook
- [ ] Credit Cards
- [ ] Detergent/Iron
- [ ] Electric Converter
- [ ] Flashlight
- [ ] Gifts
- [ ] Hangers
- [ ] Luggage Tags
- [ ] Passport/Visas
- [ ] Pens/Pencils
- [ ] Playing Cards
- [ ] Radio
- [ ] Reading Material
- [ ] Safety Pins
- [ ] Scissors
- [ ] Sewing Kit
- [ ] Stamps
- [ ] Sunglasses
- [ ] Tape Recorder
- [ ] Travel Tickets
- [ ] Traveler's Checks
- [ ] Umbrella
- [ ] Wallet

EXHIBIT X

for unexpected stops along the way to enjoy historical landmarks and spectacular views.

Finances

• Many hotels and restaurants will not accept out-of-town personal checks. So take a combination of credit cards, traveler's checks, or cash.

• Don't carry a lot of cash. What cash you do carry should be divided between husband and wife.

• Gasoline credit cards help reduce the amount of cash needed.

Car Organization

Here are a few more ideas that will help lessen the possibility of "Oops, I forget the. . ." Remember to take the following as fits your needs:

• Child's favorite blanket for napping.
• A pillow
• Towels to cover car seats and steering wheel in hot areas. They can also be used as pillows or to mop up spills.
• First-aid kit. Fill an empty coffee can with bandages, aspirin, antiseptic, thermometer, scissors, safety pins, tweezers, adhesive tape, gauze, cotton balls, and cotton swabs.
• A flashlight that works. Check the batteries before you leave home.
• A cloth drawstring bag (you can make one of these in a few minutes with some fabric scraps) to carry in the glove compartment or hang on a knob. This bag can contain such items as Handy Wipes or a damp washcloth in a plastic bag, "clean" snacks such as peanuts or gum, a daily devotional booklet, medium-sized baggies (children can use them for collectibles), a baby bib, and other miscellaneous items.

• Another bag can be hung on the back of the front seat or a car door to store play things for the children. This bag could contain crayons, scissors, glue, jump rope (for gas and rest stops), and games.

• A thermos of drinking water and paper cups. Or use a squirt bottle so the children can just squirt water into their mouths or each other's mouths.

• Bathing suits should be easily accessible, even on winter trips. Many hotels have hot tubs or heated pools.

• A camera to record your memories. It's great if you have an inexpensive camera that each child can use to take a few photos. That way he can make his own personal vacation scrapbook.

On the Road

• Picnic whenever possible. It's less expensive than fast-food stops and restaurants, and probably more nutritious.

• Remember, even baby needs a change of space and fresh air. Stop for a quick walk with the baby, or unfold the stroller and take a short, brisk walk. For driver safety and children's sanity, some sort of stop should be made every two hours.

• Depending on the age of your children, give them their own map so they can follow the route and tell you how far it is to the next town or stop.

• Provide pad and pencil for each child so he can keep a journal of the trip. Crayons are good, too, for illustrating what they see and do.

• One way to maintain order in the car is to give each child a bag filled with pennies, nickels, or dimes at the start of the vacation. Mom and Dad begin the vacation with an empty bag (no, not an empty wallet!). Each time a child is disobedient or naughty in some way, he must give up a coin from his bag and put it in the parent's bag. Any money the children have at the end of the trip is theirs to keep.

One last thing. Always take along a sense of humor! You can count on something going wrong. If you can laugh a little, it will help ease the tension.

After the vacation, plan a "remember when" evening. Review the movies, photos, scrapbooks, and journal. If the grandparents or friends are coming over, have each family member prepare to show and tell his or her favorite part of the trip. The memories are an important part of a vacation. I hope your family will have many wonderful memories.

Chapter 18 | Travel Smart— Automobile Organization

"I sought the Lord, and He answered me, and delivered me from all my fears."

Psalm 34:4 NASB

So many women today are responsible for their own cars. To maximize our safety, I've prepared a checklist of practical items to keep in the car, plus a few things to do to prevent or minimize problems. You can't be too careful in this area, so travel smart.

Here are the things you should keep in your glove compartment:

- Maps
- Notepad and pen
- Tire pressure gauge
- Handy wipes
- Sunglasses
- Mirror (this can be kept above the sun visor)
- Extra pair of nylon hose for that unexpected run
- Reading material—especially a pocket size Bible so you can enjoy prayer and Bible reading during waiting times in the car.

- Can opener
- Plastic fork and spoon
- Change for phone calls (or tolls if you live in certain parts of the country)
- Business cards
- Band-Aids
- Matches
- Stationery—again, waiting can be used constructively to catch up on correspondence
- Scissors, nail clippers
- Children's books and/or games

And here are a few more things to keep in your trunk. Many of them can be put in a shoe box and stored neatly in the trunk. Or a plastic dishpan serves well and can also be used to carry water in an emergency:

- Authorized empty gas can
- Fuses
- Jumper cables
- Flares
- Screwdriver
- Extra fan belt and spark plugs
- Flashlight (check the batteries periodically)
- First-aid kit
- Fire extinguisher—there are small ones made especially for automobiles
- Instructions on how to change a tire
- Blanket/towel
- Chains—for winter months
- Snow scraper
- Rope

Protect Your Car

- Hide a key in case you ever lock your keys inside

the car. (Caution: Don't put the key under the hood if you have an inside hood release.)

• Print your name, address, and phone number on a 3'' x 5'' card (or use your business card) and slide it down your car window frame on the driver's side. If your car is ever lost or stolen, this will help you prove the auto is yours.

• If you live in a potentially snowy area, keep a bag of kitty litter in your trunk. This will help you get traction if you're ever stuck in snow.

• Your rubber car mats can be used to prevent your windshield from freezing. Put them on the outside of the windows and use the wipers to hold them in place. If there's snow or ice, you won't have to scrape.

• Your car may not start if your battery terminals become corroded. Simply scrub them with a mixture of one cup baking soda and two cups water. It cleans them right up!

• You might want to have a rechargeable, battery-run hand vacuum to keep the car interior clean.

• If you aren't mechanically inclined, then you'd be wise to find a qualified mechanic you can trust, preferably one who has developed a good reputation. Keep your car well-serviced. Follow your maintenance manual for regular oil changes and tune-ups. Check the tires every 5,000 miles to make sure the tread is not wearing low.

A car, like our homes, reflects who we are. A well-maintained, organized, and clean (inside and out) automobile can reduce a lot of stress in our lives. It doesn't take long each week to maintain our cars. And we will benefit in the long run when we trade it in or sell it.

Chapter 19 | You're Moving... Again?

My friend Marcia is married to a lieutenant in the U.S. Army. About the time she finally unpacks the last box and begins to feel somewhat acclimated to her new home, her husband announces, "It's time to pack up. We're moving next month." In the past 11 years, Marcia has moved 11 times.

Most women find the prospect of moving about as exciting as changing several messy diapers each day. It's usually not something we're eager to do. However, the fact is that most of us move on an average of once every three years. So it is a part of many of our lives. And if we've preplanned and organized, moving can be a fairly easy and smooth process.

Before we review our checklist, there are two questions we must have answered:

1) How long do we have to plan our move? Is it a week? A month? Six months? Our checklist can be

adjusted to any time frame, but with a shorter period we need to set more rigid deadlines for each aspect of the list.

2) How are we going to move? Will this be a "do it ourselves" move, or will we hire a moving company, or do a combination of both?

Once we've established when and how we're moving, we are ready to begin.

Step 1: Household Check-off List

There are so many details to remember before moving time that it's easy to forget important things until it's too late. These are essential details that should be taken care of before the moving van arrives.

TRANSFER OF RECORDS

- School records
- Auto registration
- Driver's license
- Bank accounts
- Medical and dental records
- Eyeglass and contact prescriptions
- Pet immunization records
- Legal documents
- Church and other organization memberships
- Insurance

SERVICES TO DISCONTINUE

- Telephone
- Electric, gas, water, and other utilities

- Layaway purchases
- Cleaners—pick up up all your clothes before the move
- Milk delivery
- Fuel delivery
- Cable television
- Pest control
- Water softener or bottled water
- Garbage pickup
- Diaper service

CHANGE OF ADDRESS NOTIFICATION

- Local post office
- Magazines
- Friends and relatives
- Insurance companies
- Creditors and charge accounts
- Lawyer
- Church

Step 2: *Preparing for Moving Day*

- Reserve a moving company, if needed.
- Enlist some volunteers for moving day. Neighbors or friends from the church are potential candidates and usually are very willing to help.
- Collect boxes from local supermarkets and drugstores. Be sure to go to stores early in the day before boxes are flattened and tossed. Or ask the manager to save you a few boxes. Some moving companies will loan you special containers such as wardrobe boxes. Perfect boxes are also great for moving because they are standardized and have handles for easy lifting.
- Buy felt-tip marking pens to color code your boxes. (More about this later.)

- Prepare a work area, such as a card table, that can be used for wrapping and packing.
- Clean and air out the refrigerator and kitchen range.
- Make sure gas appliances are properly disconnected.
- Make a list of items that require special care when being packed—your antique lamp, or a china cup and saucer collection.
- Empty gas tanks on mowers and chain saws and discard all flammable materials.
- Leave an open space in the driveway or on the street for the truck, trailer, or moving van.
- Keep a small box of tools handy to dismantle furniture.
- Keep a bucket, rags, and cleaning products ready for a final cleaning of the home after it is empty.

Step 3: Packing

This is probably the most important part of your move. Proper packing and identification of your containers can assure that none of your belongings are damaged or lost.

- Use sturdy boxes for packing. Fruit and liquor boxes often have extra reinforcement and are good for heavy items like books. In addition, have a generous supply of padding. Packing paper can be purchased at low cost at your local newspaper plant or a local moving company. This unprinted paper is excellent for wrapping dishes and glassware. (Ink from newspapers will stain many of your items.)
- Begin packing, if possible, two weeks before moving day.
- Use colored pens or a number system to mark each box, identifying its contents and the room where it is to go. Examples:

Yellow—Kitchen
Green—Garden and garage
Blue—Brad's bedroom

Or number boxes and make out 3'' x 5'' cards, using the system we described in Chapter 5. Make out one card for every box, and list on the card what is in the box and in which room it belongs. Put your cards in a small box to carry with you to your new home. There you can direct each box to the appropriate room by quick reference to the box number and your cards.

Because you know by your numbered cards what is in each box without opening the box, you can unpack priority items first. This is also a great way to organize things you plan on storing in the basement or attic of your new home.

• Moving is a good way to weed out things you no longer need or use. While some items should be thrown away, others such as old clothing can be donated to churches, orphanages, or the Salvation Army. Or if you have time, run an ad in the local paper, or hold a garage sale. Remember that when you give items away to non-profit organizations, you can use the net value as a deduction from your income tax. Be sure to get a signed receipt.

• Don't put fragile and heavy items together in the same box.

• Use smaller boxes for heavier items and larger boxes for lightweight bulky items.

• Fill each box completely and compactly. Don't over or under fill.

• When packing glass dishes, put a paper plate between each plate as a protector. Stack plates on end—not flat. They seem to travel better packed that way.

• Popcorn (not the real kind) is another good packaging agent for china cups and crystal glasses. Fill the cups and glasses with popcorn before wrapping in unprinted paper. Foam padding also works well to protect breakables.

• To protect mirrors and paintings, cut heavy cardboard to fit around them, bind with tape, and label "FRAGILE."

• Remove legs, if possible, from tables and pack them on edge. If that is not feasible, load tables with their surface down and legs up. Protect a wood finish with blankets or other padding.

• Furniture pads can be wrapped around items like lamps and tied together, or sewn together temporarily with heavy thread.

• Seal boxes with heavy-duty packing tape. Or put the boxes into trash bags and then tape.

• Move dresser drawers with the clothes inside.

• When removing medicines and cleaning agents from the bathroom, make sure they are packed and sealed immediately so small children cannot reach them.

Step 4: Loading the Van, Truck, or Trailer

• Park next to the widest door of your home, leaving enough room to extend a ramp.

• Load the vehicle one quarter section at a time, using all the space from floor to ceiling. Put heaviest items in the front half of the vehicle. Try to load weight evenly from side to side to prevent shifting.

• Tie off each quarter with rope. This prevents your items from banging against each other and keeps the load from shifting.

• Use a dolly for heavy items. This can be rented from a moving company or rental store.

• CAUTION: When lifting heavy objects, bend your knees and use your leg muscles. Keep your back as straight as possible.

- Fit bicycles and other odd-shaped items along the walls of the truck, or on top of stacked items.
- When everything is loaded, finish cleaning your house, lock the door, and you're on your way!

20 | *Family Conference Time*

"Be subject to one another in the fear of Christ."

Ephesians 5:21 NASB

Probably the number one question women ask me at the More Hours in My Day seminars is, "How do I get my husband and children involved?" That's a difficult question to answer because each family is different. However, in this day of changing roles in our society, it is very important that we have a common understanding within our families about what needs to be accomplished, and who will do it. Most of us no longer live in a time when Mom takes care of the inside of the house and Dad takes care of earning the money. Conflict arises when we don't recognize that changes are taking place.

One mistake many women make is that they assume everyone understands his or her roles. They never discuss their expectations with their husband or children. With many mothers working, it is often necessary for other family members to assume some of the responsibilities that once were traditionally the woman's. The family needs to understand the concept of TEAM. Discipline, sacrifice, and investment of time are required as team members strive to "win." The coach and captain aren't the only players that make a winning team. Mom isn't the only player in the family—everyone has a valuable part. So I first recommend that moms stop carrying the whole team. That only leads to tired, burned-out, frustrated women.

It didn't take the Barnes family long to realize we needed a regular, set time to discuss important topics. Since one of our long-range goals was to raise independent children who were responsible teenagers, Bob and I felt one way to achieve this goal was to allow them to be part of the decision-making process. When someone is allowed to help make decisions, he or she is more likely to share the responsibility.

But how could we set aside more time when everyone was already busy with many activities? Our solution also resolved another chronic problem in our home. Probably the most hectic time for our family was Sunday morning before church. Mom and Dad often had a few cross words because we were late. Breakfast was hurried. Mom couldn't get dressed until the children's hair was combed. The children were crying because of a disagreement. By the time we drove into the church parking lot, we were rarely in a mood for worship. All in all, Sundays were strained times.

In order to solve our two problems—stressful Sundays and the need for family meetings—we decided to start going out for breakfast on Sunday mornings before church. Overnight we saw an improvement. This eliminated the problem of food preparation and cleanup. It was an opportunity to teach our children the social graces. And it gave us time to discuss various aspects of our family life. We established Sunday breakfasts as part of our regular monthly budget, and all of us looked forward to these times together.

Over the years, we changed our family meetings from Sunday breakfasts to Friday evening activities, and then back again to Sunday breakfasts. Mom and Dad often discussed topics to be reviewed beforehand, but there was also opportunity for any child to place a specific item on the agenda. This process helped our family become a team.

These meetings were often opened to friends. We let our children take turns inviting a friend to join our family. This gave us an opportunity to meet our children's friends and allowed them to meet us. Occasionally a whole family would join us. This was a great time to share our Christian faith, and often they were our guests at church.

Sometimes we planned various family activities at these breakfasts. While we continued the eating out tradition, we could have accomplished the same goal in many other ways. Family conferences and fun can be combined in such activities as:

- Make a collage on love
- Make and fly kites
- Assemble puzzles
- Write and produce a play
- View family movies or videos.
- Have family celebrations
- Exercise together
- Have a make-up party
- Visit a local industry
- Have a fix-it night

- Make a terrarium
- Write letters to grandparents
- Cook and bake

- Make and sail a boat
- Play board games
- Tell stories
- Put on a puppet show
- Go on picnics

- Model clay

- Ride bicycles
- Play charades
- Visit a farm
- Have discussions and debates
- Have a fire drill
- Make Christmas ornaments
- Make candles

There are many more family activities; we're limited only by our imagination. Our family activities and conference times played a valuable part in establishing harmony, respect, and pride in our family unit. Not every meeting and activity was a success, but we usually gained greater respect for our family members. When the children got older, we often ended the time by having each person mention his or her needs so we could pray specifically for each other during the next week.

Family Work Planner

There is no reason why Mom must continue to pick up after everyone in the home. We had a motto in our family: "Anything you mess up, you clean up." This little saying saved all of us many hours of double duty, and gave us time to go camping, fishing, to the museum, or to the beach, rather then being strapped to the house on weekends.

One idea that helped us to distribute the work load around the house was to write on separate slips of paper the chores that needed to be done each week. We placed these slips in a basket and every Saturday each of us drew one or more slips and learned our responsibilities for the next week. As each assignment was drawn, it was recorded on a Daily Work Planner (see Exhibit Y) which was posted in a conspicuous place. Each family member was responsible to complete his assignment. Mom and Dad also drew, for this was a team effort. Everyone helped meet the responsibilities of the family.

If you have a wide range of ages in your home, you might want to use two baskets—one for the smaller children and one for the rest of the family. That way the little children don't draw jobs that are too difficult. It is also important that Mom and Dad inspect to make sure the chores are done properly. Remember, "It's not

DAILY WORK PLANNER DATE _March 23-29_

DAY OF WEEK	MOM	DAD	#1 CHILD	#2 CHILD	#3 CHILD	#4 CHILD	#5 CHILD
SATURDAY	— Clean out the garage — McDonalds - 6:00 PM						Feed Dog
SUNDAY	Church — Family						↑
MONDAY	Laundry		Clean bedrm.			Fold Clothes	Feed Dog
TUESDAY	ironing	set out trash	Rake Leaves	Rake Leaves	Rake Leaves		→
WEDNESDAY	House Work		Vacuum House			Dust W/MOM	
THURSDAY		Wash Car		Help Wash Car			
FRIDAY	Laundry	set out trash	Mow lawn	Sweep walk-ways	water plants		

what you expect, but what you inspect'' that teaches children to be responsible family members. Occasionally, to help build good team morale, give a special reward if the children have done a good job for several weeks.

Please note that I am not suggesting that children assume the load in maintaining a house. As parents we must be sensitive to our children's own activities. They need time to participate in sports, music, homework, and other school and church activities. We want to let them experience being a child. At the same time, there are responsibilities that they have as members of a family. We need to work together so no one family member has too heavy a load.

Sometimes the family unit has to pitch in for special occasions—when company is coming, cleaning the garage, a garage sale, etc. Sometimes one family member's needs are more important than the others at that time. We need to learn to make those value judgments, and we can by being sensitive to the needs of everyone in the family.

We also need to recognize our priorities in relating to our mate and children. When my children were still at home, I often remembered, ''You were a wife to your husband before you were a mother to your children.'' The children will grow up and leave home (hopefully). However, we will still have our mates. We don't want to wake up one morning after the children are raised and think, ''Who am I?'' So a couple needs to spend quality time with each other without the children. We must not use the excuse that we can't afford it. We can't afford not to. Bob and I have planned times together and put them on our calendar just as we would any other appointment. We protect those times and don't cancel unless there is a real emergency.

For single women who are raising children alone, the pressures are even more intense, especially when the children are young. I believe the family conference time and division of responsibilities can help relieve some of the pressure. However sometimes as women, whether married or single, we may have to leave some things undone rather than continue to tax our own spirit and become burned-out. One question we can learn to ask is "Will it matter in five years?" If not, maybe it's not that important today.

There are no rules on how a home should be run. In this book I have tried to provide a few ideas in areas where many of us struggle. But each family needs to set its own standards. My family has loved working together as we set joint goals. But it's a process that takes time and everyone must learn new ways of cooperating.

In his first letter, the apostle Peter wrote that wives could influence their husbands "even if any of them are disobedient to the word, they may be won without a word by the behavior of their wives" (1 Peter 3:1 NASB). Even though Peter was talking about salvation, he gives an excellent principle. In our society, the mother sets the tone for the family and home. Many times husbands and children are not as excited about the home as we are. If we are aware of this truth, we can live with fewer disappointments because we have fewer expectations.

We need to remember that it is not our role to change our husband and children. God will do that in His time. We must be faithful to the Scriptures and love our family even when they may not return that love. What we need to recognize is that there are many areas of stress that we *can* relieve. I have attempted to give some practical helps in many of those areas. Implementing these organizational techniques can help us enjoy more hours in our day and experience more joy in our home.

In short, this is a recipe for survival for busy women.

"More Hours in My Day" can provide many of the organizational materials that are recommended in this book. You may obtain a price list by sending your request and a self-addressed envelope to:

More Hours in My Day
2838 Rumsey Drive
Riverside, CA 92506